DAISY UP...BEGIN YOUR DAY IN GOD'S EMBRACE

A 30 DAY JOURNEY

MARYKAY MOORE

Xulon
PRESS

TABLE OF CONTENTS

DEDICATION

To all my spiritual daughters past, present, and to come. May you continue to grow and deepen your relationship with God. I love and cherish you forever!

ACKNOWLEDGEMENTS

I've been greatly blessed to have many friends walk this journey with me. Writing a book is a perilous adventure in itself. There are lots of peaks and valleys in the process and I've needed strength and encouragement to keep pressing on toward the goal. I thank each and every one of you for your prayers and support. I want to thank my sisters, Gloria Prendergast and Maggie Mansfield for being my cheerleaders and promoters. I thank my writing group and Kris Ferguson who kept me on task in writing each week. I want to thank Ryan Ford who skillfully helped me with the graphics. I am elated that once again my sister Gloria Prendergast created and drew my cover design. I am so grateful, Sis. I especially thank Jill Hardie, Stefanie Libertore, Kim Dent, and Cleta Scarbrough , who read my manuscript and blessed me with their kind endorsements. But most of all, I thank my Father in Heaven, for giving me His grace and strength to write this book for His honor, glory, and praise!

ENDORSEMENTS

*D*aisy Up is a great way to go deeper with God. Each day will awaken the soul with relevant scripture, probing questions and practical action steps. Marykay's easy-to-read style invites the reader on a journey of knowing God and His transforming love. It's a refreshing and significant way to *Daisy Up!*
Stefanie Libertore Client Services Director for the Pregnancy Support Center in Canton, Ohio

Reading *Daisy Up* was like getting together with Life Coach Marykay Moore over coffee for an honest discussion about the issues that shape us as wives, mothers and friends. Through her wisdom and thought-provoking questions, she encouraged me to embrace the blessings, challenges and virtues God uses to shape our character, and bring us true joy. I love that each day only takes a few minutes to read, but if I have a little more time, there are journal prompts and Daisy Up exercises that enrich the journey. As my personal Life Coach, Marykay has brought me into a new, loving relationship with God. I can hardly wait to share this remarkable book with the women in my life so they too can experience that there's no better way to start the day than to *Daisy Up.*

Jill Hardie Author of the *The Sparkle Box—A Gift With The Power to Change Christmas*

Marykay Moore is a woman of wisdom who has a gift of writing and speaking on God's Word in such a way that you can immediately make a connection and apply it to your life. This book-*Daisy Up*- is a beautiful mini-series of teaching with scripture that speaks to the heart. A daily devotional that is thought provoking and is sure to take you to the next level with God.

Cleta Scarbrough Director of Women's Ministry at High Mill Church of the Resurrection in Canton, Ohio

Marykay Moore has packed years of godly wisdom, relevant questions and powerful action steps into bite sized nuggets. *Daisy Up* is like a daily vitamin for your soul that provides the perfect dose of encouragement, enlightenment and attitude adjustment for your day. Whether you're feeling a little droopy or just need a nudge towards God's embrace, you won't be disappointed. There's a new buzz word in town—read on, and while you're at it, *Daisy Up.*

Kim Dent Women's ministry and retreat speaker

INTRODUCTION

*D**aisy Up?** What does that mean? As I pondered this question, words began to pop up in my mind like tiny marbles in a pin ball machine. Words like…*get up, perk up, wake up, buck up, look up, and step up.* Instantly, **wake up**, stood out like a neon light. It sounded like a clarion call to awaken each day, like a daisy, allowing myself to unfold in God's embrace.

"He awakens me morning by morning, wakens my ear to listen like one being taught." Isaiah 50:4

A morning quiet time is a practice I've observed most of most of my life, and I felt this was a heartwarming way to pass it on to others. Perhaps, *Daisy Up,* will be the new buzz word for our quiet time with God. Strangely, this title came to me in the middle of a writing prompt. One of my characters turned out to be a homeless destitute girl living on the streets in a cardboard box. Her name was *Daisy*. One afternoon a kind lady walked down her street and reached out to her in love. She encouraged Daisy to look up and hope for a better tomorrow, promising to help her find a new life. In that moment, I knew the title of my book would be *Daisy Up*. I wanted to be that woman who begins her day in God's embrace and brings the promise of new hope and encouragement to those living in cardboard boxes of despair, shame, and hopelessness or to those just needing to know that God loves and cares for them.

What about you? Do you hear the clarion call too? Do you want to wake up allowing yourself to gently unfold in God's embrace? Do you want to *daisy up* to what God is speaking to you each day? He will reveal it to you through your quiet time with him each morning. Each day of **Daisy Up** is a shortened reflection from my sermon files. I have prayed for everyone who will hold this book in their hands. I've prayed that you are receptive and eager to begin your day awakening to His voice. The practice of setting aside a quiet time with the Lord has changed and transformed my life and it will do the same for you. This is a 30 day journey but you can go through it at your own pace. You are free to use this book any way you wish. You can do it in the order it is written or pick and choose your reflection for the day. You can do it on a retreat, with a friend, or in a small group. There is no right or wrong way to journey through this book. Nor do you have to agree with everything written in these pages. Accept the things you like and disregard the others. Ask the Holy Spirit to lead you into an encounter with God that will radically transform your life. How about it? Shall we *Daisy Up* together? If you're ready, let's take a stroll down Daisy Lane.

DAY 1

DAISY UP…EMBRACING HOPE

*"We have this hope as an anchor
for the soul, firm and secure."*
Heb.6:19

D o you remember the story of Daisy from the introduction to this book? She was a homeless teenage girl, destitute and alone, living on the streets in a tattered cardboard box. I can only imagine the sense of hopelessness that held her captive as she struggled to survive from one day to the next. Then one afternoon in the midst of her despair, a kind lady gave her a reason to hope once again. How many times have you asked yourself the question, "Is there any hope?" Hope, at times, seems nebulous: one day you've grasped hold of it and the next you see it slipping away without a backward glance. How does that happen? Why do we lose our focus and give in to despair?

How many women do you know who are living in cardboard boxes of shame, desperation, and despondency wearing the cloak of hopelessness? Do you hear their prayer, "God, is there any hope for me? Is my life worth living?" Are you one of those women? What is your prayer? What's the name on your card-board box? Write it in the box below:

```
God, is there any hope for me?
My cardboard box is...
```

I've heard it said that we can go forty days without food, three days without water, eight minutes without air, but we can't go a single second without hope. When hope is gone, you're like a dead person walking. As a Life Purpose Coach, I've seen many women who feel like they are beyond hope. One of my greatest joys is to tell them it's never too late. Hope is within reach if they will BELIEVE.

Hope makes all the difference. When you have hope, you are capable of bearing extraordinary burdens. You can be victorious even when the odds are stacked against you. Hope is putting faith in action where doubting might be easier. Albert Einstein said, "Learn from yesterday, live for today, hope for tomorrow."

Hope for tomorrow. What is Hope? The dictionary defines hope as expectation, desire, confidence, longing, and anticipation. It is a yearning for something wonderful to happen. Some people think it can be found in a pill, an alcoholic drink, a night of frivolity, fame, success, or in the accumulation of worldly possessions. In the end, they are usually disappointed and disillusioned. The world does not have the answers. So what does the Bible tell us about hope?

"Put your hope in God." Ps.42:5

"And hope does not disappoint us, because God has poured out his love into our hearts by the Holy Spirit, whom he has given us." Ro.5:5

"Christ in you, the Hope of Glory." Col.1:27

"Against all hope, Abraham in hope believed." Ro.4:18

Why do you need HOPE?

- You need hope to believe that God will work in your lives.
- You need hope to believe that God can change your circumstances.
- You need hope to believe that God will meet you where you are.

- You need hope to believe that God will supply all your needs.
- You need hope to believe that God will work all things out for your good.

"Of all things beyond salvation, people are most desperate for hope." Florence Littauer

The image of an anchor takes me back to a time when my husband purchased a used six passenger boat. It conjures up memories of fun, laughter, and excitement. We hauled that boat out to Lake Milton with our grandchildren, relatives and friends. In the middle of the day, we steered the boat over to our favorite scraggy island. There my husband lowered the anchor to the lake's floor as we disembarked for a time of eating, swimming, and exploring. We never worried when the high waves of passing motorboats caused our little vessel to rock from side to side. The anchor held it fast and secure.

How are you feeling today? Is your anchor secure or have you lost your bearings? Are you feeling unhinged and apprehensive? Do you feel like you are adrift on the sea of no return? Do you realize you don't have to stay there—that you are not alone? Jesus came for the lost and weary. He is here for you now, calling you to shore. Despite all the trials and uncertainties in your life, the winds of change and the overwhelming sense of discouragement, Jesus is your anchor and He will keep you safe and secure. Now take a little time to strengthen your hope in the exercises below.

Daisy up Exercises:

Write ***Heb.6:19*** in the box below and draw an image of an anchor. Print the name of Jesus on the anchor.

Where do you need HOPE right now? Circle any that apply.

marriage	health	salvation	forgiveness
relationships	finances	family	overcoming addiction
elderly parents	job	career	food, clothing, shelter
housing	teenagers	babies	your studies

Other:

Journal Prompt:

Write a letter to God about one of the areas you circled above. Speak to him from your heart. Tell him what it is and how you are feeling about it. Ask him to speak to you and guide you in the way you are to go. Ask him to calm your heart and restore hope to your soul.

I encourage you to crawl out of your cardboard box today. *Daisy up in God's Embrace and receive the gift of Hope.* You are a Daughter of the King, you belong in a palace.

Prayer:

Heavenly Father, I came before you today desperate and alone, needing hope for my weary soul. You have seen my tears and heard my cry. You reached out to me and held me in your embrace. Thank you for the whispers of love and the promise of hope for a better tomorrow. I am rising up out of the ashes- out of my cardboard box- because You, Lord, are my Hope and my Anchor. Amen.

Quote:

"Most of the important things in the world have been accomplished by people who have kept on trying when there seemed to be no hope at all." Dale Carnegie

Day 2

DAISY UP...EMBRACING A RENEWED MIND

"Be transformed by the renewing of your mind."

Ro.12:2

I' ve always loved New Year's Day because it invites me to a fresh start and a new beginning. Usually on New Year's Eve, I make a list of all the major things that occurred during the past year. I read each one aloud as I thank God for the blessings and opportunities that came my way. Many of them shaped and strengthened my character in ways I never imagined. Then I look forward with hope and expectation to what the New Year will bring. For some of you, a New Year may ring in some long-awaited hopes and dreams such as:

- Preparing for a baby on its way.
- Getting married.
- Beginning a new job.
- Graduating from high school or college.
- Celebrating your first driver's license.
- Going on a mission trip.
- Meeting your soul mate.
- Getting your book published.
- Developing new talents in art, music, or dance.
- Bringing a pet into your family.
- Receiving a long-awaited promotion.

For others, this year may ring in some difficult challenges such as:

- Becoming an empty nester.
- Facing a difficult decision.
- Dealing with a chronic or terminal illness.
- Caring for aging parents.
- Ending a significant relationship.
- Grieving the loss of a loved one.
- Losing your job.
- Declaring bankruptcy.
- Moving from your home state and leaving your friends behind.

Some of us may question and wonder what the New Year will bring. While others make staunch resolutions that they believe will change their lives. A young boy asked his father what his New Year's resolution was and the father said he wanted to do everything possible to make his mother happy. The boy then asked his mother what her New Year's resolution was and she said it was to do everything possible to help his dad keep his resolution. F.M. Knowles said, "He who breaks a resolution is a weakling. He who makes one is a fool." What kind of resolutions do people make? Did you know the number one resolution in America is losing weight? Others are…

- Spending more time at the gym.
- Spending more time with family and friends.
- Trying to quit smoking.
- Enjoying life more.
- Learning something new.
- Helping others more.
- Cutting back on television.
- Getting organized.
- Attending a bible study.
- Being more neighborly.

A few weeks later we ask ourselves, "What was I thinking?" I believe it's critical how we approach a New Year. Do we shrug it off as just another year, or another day to celebrate? Perhaps you might consider asking God to help you Renew Your Mind in this New Year.

"Do not conform any longer to the pattern of this world, but be transformed by the renewing of your mind. Then you will be able to test and approve what God's will is—his good, pleasing and perfect will." Ro.12:2

You can ask God to transform you into a new person by changing your mind. Being transformed is a remarkable thing. Consider the caterpillar becoming a butterfly or a tadpole becoming a frog. It doesn't happen overnight, it's a gradual change that happens on the inside. When the caterpillar is finally changed into a butterfly, it becomes what God intended it to be. The same is true of us. We are being transformed into Christ and that too doesn't happen overnight. It's a slow process that happens by the renewing of your mind. Did you know that *renewing the mind* means changing on the inside? As hard as it is to change on the outside, it seems much harder to change on the inside. If there's anything we know about human nature, it is that people change slowly, if they change at all. Take a moment to think about the struggles and tensions in your life right now. If you could change anything about yourself on the inside—what would it be? Circle ones that apply to you.

- An impatient spirit.
- A critical spirit.
- A negative attitude.
- Envy and jealousy.
- Discontentment.
- Pride.
- Prejudice.
- Depression.
- Inability to say no.
- An ungrateful spirit.
- Low self-esteem.
- Seeking the approval of others.
- An unforgiving spirit.
- Resentment.
- Addictions.
- Guilt or regret.
- Greed.
- Comparing yourself to others.
- Blaming others.
- Playing the victim.

Maybe I'm an idealist, but I sincerely believe that most of us want to change something. I've watched the faces of thousands of people around the world as they wait for the ball to drop ushering in the New Year. They are all hoping for a better tomorrow.

They are tired of going around the same mountain year after year. They hope this year will be different.

> *"Forget the former things; do not dwell on the past. See I am doing a new thing. Now it springs up- do you not perceive it?" Isa.43:18-19*

Circle the word *new in the verse above.* That's the key to a fresh start. Do you believe that God wants to do a new thing in your life? What would it look like?

GOD IS THE GOD OF NEW BEGINNINGS...

He gives us a new heart. Ezek.11:19

He has made us a new creation. 2 Cor. 5:17

He gives us new life. Acts 5:20

He gives us a new command. 1 Jn. 2:8

He puts a new song in our hearts. Ps. 40:3

He renews us with His Spirit. Ezek.18:31

He renews our strength. Isa. 57:10

His mercies are new every morning. La. 3:23

We need to let go of the old and welcome in the new. We do that by renewing our mind. Did you know that your mind can be a junkyard or a treasure chest depending on what you feed it?

Are you feeding it trash or the Word of God? Did you know that your mind can work for you or against you? When it's working for you, it helps you stay positive, reach your goals, find your purpose, think kind thoughts, and serve others. When it works against you, it keeps you negative and discouraged. These are landmines that keep you from accomplishing your purpose in life. You allow yourself to think self-defeating thoughts, which are the tools of the devil. He wants to control us and keep us from fulfilling our God-given destiny. That's why it is critical to **keep on renewing your mind.** Write that phrase in the space below:

The dictionary definition for renew is: To begin again; to be restored; to become new; to bring back an original condition of freshness and vigor. A few synonyms are: renovate—which means to make good any dilapidated or damaged thing. Restore—which means to bring back to its former place or position, to restore something which has faded, vanished, or been lost. Which one describes you today?

Do you need to begin again?
Do you need to be restored to your original freshness and vigor?
Do you need to repair your mind, body, and spirit?
Do you need to restore what has been lost?

Perhaps you've succumbed to some pathetic thinking. Perhaps you've walked down the road of compromise. Perhaps you've strayed from the principles and values you once cherished. Perhaps you're doing things that are morally wrong—drugs, pornography, gambling, lying, cheating, stealing, or abusing others. Perhaps you're hanging out with the wrong crowd. Perhaps you've given up on God, your church, family, and friends.

"Yet I hold this against you; you have forsaken your first love." Rev.2:4

Where do you need to be renewing your mind? What steps can you take to keep your mind fixed on Christ and to believe that His plan for you is a future full of hope? We can't transform our mind in our own strength, we can only do it with the help of the Holy Spirit. His power will transform us into Christ Jesus. Don't give up on yourself and don't give up on others. God is for us! So let's resolve to *renew our minds* with gusto! This will happen as we develop a deeper, more intimate relationship with God.

Renewing your mind will lead to:

Renewing your personal life, goals, dreams, desires, and purpose. Renewing your marriage and family life.

Renewing your faith.

Renewing your desire to serve those in need

Renewing your ability to let go of the things that distract you from God.

Renewing your mind does not happen overnight. It is a slow and painstaking process. But the end result is like walking in the light. You see things more clearly and make better choices. This is your life. You can decide how you are going to live it. Make it count for something!

Daisy up Exercises:

In the first column list negative feedback you give yourself. In the second column take that negative comment and make it into a positive faith statement. I'll do the first one for you:

Negative Talk   *Positive Talk*

1. I can't do this project   I can do all things in Christ

2.

3.

4.

Write out the following scriptures and say them aloud.

Ro.12:2

Eph.4:23

Col.3:2

Rev.2:23

Journal Prompt:

It's important to renew my mind because… These are the steps I will take to renew my mind and heart for this New Year…

Prayer

Heavenly Father, help me to renew my mind in Christ Jesus and to believe that you have a perfect plan and purpose for my life. I want to put on the mind of Christ and live in his truth and in his love. Help me to change in the areas that are not consistent with Christ- like living. Help me to change any negative self-talk into positive Bible promises. I want to fix my mind and heart on Christ Jesus and to look forward to a future full of hope. This is my earnest prayer. Amen.

Quote:

"No matter how carefully you plan your goals, they will never be more than pipe dreams unless you pursue them with gusto." *W.Clement Stone*

Day 3

DAISY UP…EMBRACING CONTENTMENT

"I have learned the secret of being
content in any and every situation."
Phil.4:12

*W*hen was the last time you woke up feeling discontented, irritable, or cranky? Was it today, yesterday, or last week? Does it come upon you quickly and last longer than you wish. No one wants to begin their day signing a discontentment card, but we can allow it to creep in because of our circumstances, relationships, or choices we have made.

One of my favorite stories is about a rich man who was annoyed to find a fisherman sitting lazily by his boat. He asked the fisherman why he wasn't out fishing. The fisherman said he caught enough for the day. The rich man then asked why he didn't get more than he needed. The fisherman asked what he would do with them. Somewhat annoyed, the rich man told him he could earn more money, buy a bigger boat, catch more fish, have a fleet of boats, and be rich like him. The fisherman nodded and asked what he would do then? The rich man replied that he could sit down and enjoy his life. The fisherman, looking contentedly out to sea, asked, "What do you think I'm doing now?"

Unfortunately, too many people think that if they had more money or if their circumstances were different, they would be happier and more satisfied. That's a myth.

A myth is an untruth, a falsehood or a downright lie. Let's dig deeper and look at the myth of contentment (rich man) versus the secret of contentment (fisherman).

Discontentment is a nagging sense of dissatisfaction. If we're honest with ourselves, we think if certain things were different in our lives, or if we hadn't made mistakes in our past, then we would be happier and more content.

Let's examine the myth of contentment more closely. Somewhere in each of our lives is an "if only." Let's consider a few scenarios from the Bible.

- Adam and Eve   If only we hadn't eaten that apple, we'd still be in Eden.

- Moses   If only I had obeyed God's command, I'd be leading the Israelites into the Promised Land.

- Miriam   If only I hadn't complained against Moses, I wouldn't have leprosy.

- Elijah   If only I hadn't killed the prophets of Baal, I wouldn't be running for my life.

- David   If only I'd gone to battle with my men, I wouldn't be in this predicament with Bathsheba.

- Peter   If only I'd heeded the Lord's warning, I wouldn't have denied him.

What about our own lives? What are the "if only's" we ask ourselves repeatedly?

___If only I were married.

___If only I weren't married.

___If only I had more money in the bank.

___If only I had kids.

___If only I had a job.

___If only I could lose 20 lbs .

___if only my parents were ill and aging.

___if only I hadn't been abused as a child.

___if only I didn't have this addiction.

___if only I had gone to college.

___if only I weren't divorced.

___if only I didn't have this chronic illness.

___if only I hadn't cheated.

___if only….write your own below and check any above that refer to you

The problem is that our "if only's" have the power to keep us miserable, downcast, and defeated. They keep us living like victims who are always powerless and blaming others for their lot in life. That's a portrait of a discontented person. Is that how you want people to describe you? Is that how you want to be remembered?

What can we learn from this? Well, for one thing, it's not wrong to desire contentment. The problem is that we look for it in all the wrong places. We are seeking for someone or something to fill the void in our life or take the pain away from our circumstances or past sin. Contentment can't be found in persons, positions, or possessions. If you look for contentment in these things, they will only lead to disappointment. They are fleeting: here today and gone tomorrow. Consider this verse from Ecclesiastes.

"I have seen all the things that are under the sun; all of them are meaningless, a chasing after the wind." Ecc.1:14

If we are not content with our present circumstances then we won't be content in any other set of circumstances. Recently, I came across a letter from Martha Washington to her friend Mercy, in which she stated that our happiness or sadness doesn't depend on our circumstances but on our dispositions. She vowed to her friend that she would be happy no matter what situation she was in.

The myth: For some reason we have been deceived into believing we would be happier and more content if our circumstances and relationships were different. Are you carrying around the seed of discontentment? Read through some signs of discontentment. Circle those that apply to you:

o Murmuring.

o Complaining.

o Whining.

o Fretting.

o Feeling sorry for yourself.

o Blaming others for your unhappiness.

o Being negative.

o Envying others.

o Giving in to addictions.

o Comparing myself to others.

Don't' be discouraged if you marked several of these. Today is a new day. You can plant new seeds of contentment in your mind and heart.

Now let's look at the Secret of Contentment. Paul tells us that contentment doesn't come naturally. Isn't that a relief? He says it is something that needs to be learned. Read the verse below and circle the word "learned."

"…for I have learned to be content whatever the circumstances. I know what it is to be in need and I know what it is to have plenty. I have learned the secret of being content in any and every situation, whether well fed or hungry; whether living in plenty or in want." Phil.4:12

Ironically, Paul is teaching us about contentment from his prison cell in Rome. Do you think you would be content in a prison cell? Paul found that peace and contentment while under arrest. How did he achieve this?

o Paul learned that his joy was found in Christ not in his circumstances.

o Paul learned that everything—the good, the bad, the ugly came from the hand of God.

o Paul learned that he couldn't always change his circumstances but he could change his response to them.

o Paul learned that God is faithful and would give us all we needed in any and all circumstances of our life.

"But whatever was to my profit,
I now consider loss for the sake of Christ." Phil.3:7

The secret of contentment comes from believing that his power and love is at work within us regardless of our circumstances.

"…and we know that in all things, God works for the good
of those who love him, according to His purpose." Ro.8:28

How do these verses speak into your own life? Have you received any new insight?

Changing circumstances and relationships do not determine my contentment. But my faith and trust in Jesus Christ have everything to do with my contentment. Trusting and waiting on God's timing in my life is essential to living in peace and contentment. Ask God for the spirit of contentment and He will give it to you freely and without measure.

Daisy up Exercises:

1. Contentment comes from gratitude.

   Take a nature walk today. Breathe in the air. Listen to the song of birds or the whisper of the wind in the trees. Notice the colors, shape and texture of the trees, flowers, and leaves. Watch the animals at play. Sit by a lake, pond, or stream and thank God for the blessings in your life.

2. Start a gratitude journal. At the end of the day jot down 5 things you are grateful for. You can even do this as a family. Put a journal or pad on the table and have each member of the family jot down one thing they are grateful for each day. This makes for great table conversation and a wonderful way to count your blessings on the feast of Thanksgiving.

Check out these scriptures:

Ps.145:16   Prov.23:4   Prov.30:8   Ecc.5:10
Write your favorite contentment scripture in the box below then memorize it so you can recall it when you begin to feel discontented.

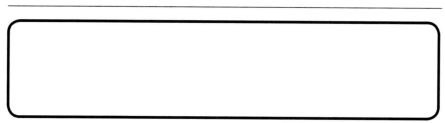

Journal Prompt:

What's your impossible situation? Where are you discontent in your life right now? Talk to God about it as honestly as possible. Write down your thoughts and feelings and ask Him to help you find contentment in Him.

Prayer:

My Lord and My God, you are my all in all. My heart belongs to you. You satisfy my every need and desire. I am content knowing that you see every single detail of my life and that you will provide everything I need to find joy and contentment in my present situation. I believe that you are walking with me, Lord, and I am content in your abiding Presence. Amen.

Quote:

"I don't want to waste any more time running after the good that is not the best." Oswald Chambers

Day 4

DAISY UP…EMBRACING GOD'S VOICE

"The Lord will guide you always."

Isa. 58:11

*I*magine yourself in a restaurant, walking down the street, attending a meeting, or watching a sports event. What is one thing many people are doing? Talking or texting on a cell phone would be a good guess. What has propelled the nation into such an obsession with cell phones? The reason is very simple— people want to be connected. Wouldn't it be amazing if people wanted to be connected like that with God on a daily basis? The truth is that He created us for that kind of deep personal relationship with Him. He wants to speak to us and he texts us in His word. Yet still, I hear the question, "How do I hear from God?" Maybe if we would turn the cell phones off we would be still enough to hear His voice. Have you had times in your life when you've felt absolutely clueless about what to do in certain situations?

- Have you found yourself trying to crawl out of a dark tunnel?
- Have you wandered through times of wilderness, doubt and confusion?
- Have you found yourself standing at the crossroads wondering which path to take?
- Have you desperately called on God to free you from addiction or sin?
- Have you sought God's guidance concerning your marriage, career, health, parenting or finances?

One thing is certain. We need to hear from God for guidance in our lives. What is guidance? Webster defines it as direction, instruction, advice, counsel, wisdom and teaching. At these critical times in our lives, we need guidance from someone we can fully trust and who has our best interests at heart. That's where God comes into the picture. Throughout the Bible we see countless stories of God's guidance:

- He guided the Israelites in the desert with a cloud by day and fire by night.

- We see the appearance of angels.
- We read of dreams and visions.
- The people were guided through prophets, judges, priests, kings.
- There were miraculous signs and wonders.
- He guided the Magi by a star.
- The Coming of the Holy Spirit.

Where are you today? Are you at a juncture in your life when you desperately need to hear from God? When you call on him He will answer you because:

GOD PROMISES TO GUIDE US

"The Lord will guide you always." Isa.58:11
"I will instruct you and teach you in the way you should go."
Ps.32:8

GOD HAS A PLAN FOR OUR LIFE

"For I know the plans I have for you, says the Lord, plans to prosper you and not to harm you, plans to give you hope and a future." Jer.29:11

"Ask and you will receive; seek and you will find; knock and the door will be opened to you." Matt.7:7

We need to ask God for counsel at all times but especially when we are making major life decisions that will not only affect us but our families and loved ones.

HOW CAN I HEAR FROM GOD?

There are many ways to hear from God but let's examine 5 simple principles that will help you hear God's voice.

1. PRAYER

Guidance will flow out of a genuine relationship with God which is accomplished through spending time in prayer. Call to mind how you relate to your best friend. You talk and listen to each other, sharing everything in your life without reservation. You feel accepted, safe, and loved. That's the kind of relationship God wants with you.

"The Lord is near to all who call on him in truth."
Ps.145:18

"Call to me and I will answer you." Jer.33:3

"Come near to God and he will come near to you."

James 4:8

2. SCRIPTURE

God's general guidance is revealed in Scripture. He gives us moral and spiritual counsel about how to live and conduct our lives. God will never ask us to do anything contrary to his Word.

"All scripture is God-breathed and is useful for teaching, rebuking, correcting, and training in righteousness so that the man of God may be thoroughly equipped for every good work." 2 Tim.3:16

God's specific guidance is not always as clear. For instance, if you are trying to decide on your career in life, the Bible will not tell you to be a nurse, teacher, or lawyer, or painter. But if you ask, God will lead you to make decisions wisely.

3. HOLY SPIRIT

Sometimes we struggle with a decision because we're not sure if it's God's will or our own desire. If we are believers, we are sealed with the Holy Spirit. He dwells within us and we need to trust in his counsel.

"But when he, the Spirit of Truth comes,
he will guide you into all truth." John 16:13

Sometimes the Holy Spirit will give you a strong desire or leaning in a particular direction. I learned long ago to *notice what you notice.* Pay attention to the way the Holy Spirit prompts and instructs you.

"For it is God who works in you to will and act according to
his good purpose." Phil.2:13

At other times, the Holy Spirit will speak to you in unusual ways such as:

- Prophecy
- Dreams
- Visions
- Angels
- Audible voice

4. COUNSEL OF PEOPLE GROUNDED IN THEIR FAITH

"The way of a fool seems right to him, but a wise man
listens to advice." Prov.12:5

After we have prayed, searched the scriptures, and listened to the Holy Spirit, the Lord will often lead us to seek counsel from godly men and women, pastors, counselors, or close friends.

5. CIRCUMSTANCES OF OUR LIFE

"In his heart a man plans his counsel, but the Lord determines his steps." Prov.16:9

We can't always control what happens to us in life because there will always be:

times of peace

times of trial

times of dryness

times of change

times of growth

times of weakness

times of strength

times of health

times of illness

times of testing

But one thing we can be sure of—God walks with us at all times.

"We know that in all things, God works for the good of those who love him, who have been called according to his purpose." Ro.8:28

In all five of these principles one thing is imperative— the condition of the HEART. God wants us to come to him with a spirit of humility and trust.

"Trust in the lord with all your heart and lean not on your own understanding; in all your ways acknowledge him and he will make your paths straight." Prov.3:5-6

Today, at this very moment, you may be struggling with a major life decision. God wants you to come to him for guidance and he wants you to place your trust in him. Embrace God's Voice and He will give you an answer at the right time and in the right place.

Daisy up Exercises:

- Go back to 2 Tim.3:16 List 4 ways the scriptures are useful:

    1.

    2.

    3.

    4.

- Write your need on a small piece of paper and fold it into 4 parts.

    Hold that paper between the palms of your hands as you pray this prayer"

Father, I am desperate for your guidance and counsel in this particular situation. I am trusting you to lead and guide me to make the right decision. Help me to come before you in confident trust and to be patient while I wait to hear from you. I ask this in Jesus name. Amen.

Journal Prompt:

Write about a time in the past when you needed to hear from God. What was the situation and how did God answer you. Be as specific as possible. Daisy up in God's embrace and hear his voice as clearly today as you did in the past. Write about how your past experience can help you now in this time of need.

Prayer:

Heavenly Father, thank you for leading and guiding me in this time of need. I'm grateful for your Word, your Holy Spirit living in me, and for trusted friends that I can lean on in troubled times. I'm reassured and confident that you will speak to me clearly and I will hear your voice deep in my soul. Keep me close to you and in the center of your will for my life. In Jesus name I pray. Amen.

Quote:

"The lover of silence draws close to God. He talks to him in secret and God enlightens him." John Climacus

Day 5

DAISY UP…
EMBRACING THE WAIT

🌹

"Wait for the Lord; be strong and take heart

and wait for the Lord."

Ps.27:14

*A*re you a rare individual who loves to wait or are you someone who avoids it at any cost? Waiting can be tiresome since we live in a world of fast food, fast lanes, and fast service. It's supposed to make life easier and more satisfying but it seems our fast technology has made us impatient and demanding. We want things faster and faster, easier and easier. If we don't get it quickly, we tap our feet, look at our watches, sigh audibly, honk the horn, or even get into a brawl. Waiting, however, is a fact of life none of us can avoid. The poet

W.H.Auden wrote, "What is most real about us all is that each of us is waiting." As we wait, the Bible tells us to call upon the Lord.

"The Lord is near to all who call upon him." Ps.145:18

What does it mean to wait? To wait means to anticipate; hope for; and expect. It means hitting the pause button as we wait for further instruction.

WAITING ON GOD IS AN ACT OF OBEDIENCE

In Scripture, God is constantly telling his people to wait. They chafe and grumble and complain just like the rest of us. What are you waiting for? (circle any that apply)

traffic	to lose weight	graduation
a letter	release from prison	marriage
a package	love	your own home
a visit	justice	to get on a team
a phone call	job	direction
vacation	relationship	deliverance
to win the lottery	acceptance	grief to end
to prove yourself	promotion	approval or praise

Other: _____

WHY DOES GOD ASK US TO WAIT?

Let's consider several reasons God asks us to wait.

1. To discover His plan and purpose for our lives

"It is good to wait quietly for the salvation of the Lord."
Lam.3:26

God does not want to tease or tantalize us. As we are waiting, he is working out the details for our ultimate good. We need to position ourselves before God and wait for his response. Let's not make the mistake of rushing ahead of God, because it never ends well. If he closes a door, then trust that he has something better waiting in the wings for you.

2. To receive supernatural strength and energy

"Those who hope in the Lord will renew their strength."
Isa.40:31

In times of waiting, we can often become faint and weary trying to hold on for dear life. We find ourselves asking, "How long O Lord?" That's when he gives us his grace and strength to do what we can't do on our own.

3. To win battles

"Wait for the Lord and He will deliver you." Prov.20:22

Timing is everything in a battle. Attacking at the wrong time or before the commander's signal, could cost you the battle or even your life. This is also true in the spiritual realm. Waiting on the Lord ensures victory and prevents us from making foolish or life-threatening mistakes.

4. To see God working on our behalf

"No ear has perceived, no eye has seen any God besides you, who acts on behalf of those who wait for him." Isa.64:4

While we wait, God is working behind the scenes on our behalf. He is never early or late, he is right on time. He always has our best interests at heart.

5. To see our faith accomplished

"…those who hope in me will not be disappointed." Isa.49:23

We'll never be embarrassed waiting on God. We need to stand our ground when others may be enticing us to move forward, instead of waiting on God. Our faith will be rewarded as we wait for the *Go Ahead* from God. He wants to see us achieve our goals, visions and dreams in this life.

WHAT ARE THE CONSEQUENCES OF NOT WAITING?

1. We get out of God's will and

   - Make impulsive decisions.
   - Act in our own strength.
   - Take control of the situation.
   - Hurry to make something happen.
   - Rush ahead of God.

2. We can bring pain and suffering to ourselves and others—our spouse, our children, our friends, family and coworkers.
3. We can lose out in our relationships, finances, and faith. Is it worth it?
4. We can miss opportunities and blessings that God had planned for our lives. God can still bless us but it may not be the best he had planned for us if we had waited. This can cause us to lose our joy and our inner peace.

HOW DO WE WAIT?

1. TRUSTING

"Trust in the Lord with all your heart and lean not on your own understanding; in all your ways acknowledge him and He will make your paths straight." Prov.3:5-6

One thing we all know is that life will bring disappointment. What we need to remember is that God is in control of our circumstances. Don't let discouragement and setbacks keep you from trusting in God. These are the times we trust him even more.

"Commit your way to the Lord; trust in him and he will do this." Ps.37:5

Tell yourself now:

- Don't quit.
- Don't ever give up.
- Don't lose hope.

2. ACTIVELY (DILIGENTLY)

"Do not leave Jerusalem, but wait for the gift my Father promised which you have heard speak about." Acts 1:4

Waiting is never passive. Waiting is never wasted time, even though we think it is. God gives us instructions through times of actively waiting. He may change our circumstances while we wait…

- He may bring about trials and conflicts as we wait.
- He may use that time to help us examine our motives.
- He may use that time to prepare us for what is ahead.

Have your prayed this prayer? Lord, give me patience. I want it right now. Patience is a virtue, possess it if you can. Seldom found in a woman, never in a man. When we are impatient and in a hurry, we need to hear that still small voice. *"Be still and know that I am God." Ps.46:10.* We need to take a deep breath and wait for his clear direction. Stay right where you are. More importantly, don't move ahead until you hear his voice clearly.

3. EXPECTANTLY

"For the revelation awaits an appointed time…though it linger, wait for it. It will certainly come and will not delay." *Hab.2:3*

We all know that we have an enemy who wants to place doubt, fear and worry in our hearts. He wants us to think that God doesn't really care. It's at times like this that we need to tell the devil to move back. Standing boldly on our faith will strengthen us to trust God more and to expect victory. Our God is able to do whatever he wants and however he wants. Nothing is impossible with God.

I encourage you to *Daisy Up* and embrace this time of waiting God has you in right now. He's doing a work in you and will bring it to completion. Be patient!

Daisy up Exercises:

- *Write in the box all the things you are waiting for…*
- *Then write your favorite scripture from this day all around the box*

- Next time you want something immediately, set a timer for 5-10 minutes and make yourself wait patiently. Jot down your feelings and what you learned from the waiting.

Journal Prompt:

Finish this exercise with your own words.

Lord, I'm waiting for _____. I know that I get anxious and _____ while waiting but I promise to _____ You and to _____that you work for my greatest _____.

Prayer:

Heavenly Father, you know my heart and see the weariness of my soul. It seems like my whole life has been a time of waiting but you've always come through for me. Teach me to continue to trust and believe in you as I wait patiently to hear from you. Father, I respect your timing and know it is perfect. I wait in eager anticipation of your answer and direction. You are all good and my heart sings your praises. Amen.

Quote:

"We must let go of the life we have planned, so as to accept the one that is waiting for us." Joseph Campbell

Day 6

DAISY UP…EMBRACING ENCOURAGEMENT

"Therefore encourage one another and build each other up, just as in fact you are doing." 1 Thess.5:11

Would the people in your life portray you as an encourager? Maybe it's your habit to speak a kind word, send a smile, or lend moral support to someone in need. Perhaps others automatically turn up on your doorstep when they need encouragement.

According to Webster's dictionary, encouragement means: urging, reassuring, motivating, supporting, helping, rallying, and building up.

"If a person's gift is encouraging, let him encourage." Ro.12:8

In the Greek that means "to come alongside of." It is coming to the aid or assistance of someone else. It implies an ability to help someone in in an area where he or she can't help themselves. Take a minute to jot down the name of someone who recently came alongside of you_____. Now write the name of someone you came alongside of _____. How did you encourage them?

Let's look at the profile of an encourager:

- An encourager looks at a person and doesn't see the problem. Instead he sees the potential and possibilities.
- An encourager doesn't look at the past. He looks at the future.
- An encourager doesn't see what is but what can be.

Encouragement is showing people that we care about them and that they are important. And the more you encourage others, the more you are encouraged.

"Let us consider how we may spur one another on toward love and good deeds. Let us not give up meeting together, as some are in the habit of doing, but let us encourage one another all the more as you see the Day approaching." Heb.10:24-25

In Acts 4:36-37, Luke gives us a good example of someone who was an encourager. His real name was Joseph, but we know him best as Barnabas, meaning the Son of Encouragement. He played an important role encouraging Paul and bridging the gap between him and the apostles. He was also a strong encourager in the life of John Mark and walked alongside him in times of confusion and doubt.

Do you want to be a Barnabas? Do you want to be remembered as someone who always gave support and encouragement? Encouragement as used in the Bible is much more intrusive than a friendly affirmation. It is more than just offering a smile, patting someone on the back, or visiting the sick, although these are admirable qualities. Consider this scenario: Perhaps you notice that your friend is going down a dangerous path and making some bad choices. What do you do? Do you tell yourself it's none of your business? Do you talk to them rather than about them? A true encourager has the ability to head someone off at the pass and avert a potential disaster. When we have the courage to do that, we don't have to badger, preach, accuse, or judge someone. We just come alongside them as an encourager.

"See to it, brothers, that none of you has a sinful, unbelieving heart that turns away from the living God.

But encourage one another daily as long as it is called today so that none of you may be hardened by sins' deceitfulness." Heb.3:12-13

Sin can lead to unbelief. We all start slipping before we stop believing. We justify and rationalize our behavior and actions. Do you recognize these words?

- Just this once.
- It's not hurting anyone else.
- I don't want to disappoint my friends.
- It's just a small thin.
- It's my life, I can do what I want.
- Nobody has to know.
- My situation is unique.

Once we give in to these pretenses, we begin to drift. We compromise our values, principles, and lifestyle. We may still come to church, attend bible studies, and even serve in various ministries. But we are heading down the path of deceitfulness. Then we begin to lose control and enter into a very dark place. Christianity is not private—it is personal and relational.

"Let your conversation be always full of grace, seasoned with salt so that you may know how to answer everyone."
Col.4:6

"Follow the way of love and eagerly desire spiritual gifts, especially the gift of prophecy…but everyone who prophesies speaks to men for their strengthening, encouragement, and comfort." 1 Co.14:1-3

Are you willing to step up to the plate and be an encourager like Barnabas? If you do, your life will be doubly blessed as the gift is returned to you.

Daisy up Exercises:

Look around you—who needs encouragement? Is it your friends, family, a church member, co-worker, or neighbor? Who is walking down the wrong path? Who is overwhelmed and burdened right now? Who is struggling in their marriage? Who is disheartened because of finances? Who is in a battle with their teens? Who is losing sleep because of their newborns? Who is isolating themself ?

Close your eyes and let God bring them to your awareness and pray for them.

Accept this as an assignment from God. Engage in the lives of people around you with true Christ-like love. Which of these actions or attitudes do you need to delete from your character when meeting with these people?

—being judgmental   —being harsh

—being critical   —being nasty

—being unloving   —being vengeful

Ask for the guidance of the Holy Spirit. Don't act as if you are perfect and have something to teach them. Above all, show them a genuine love of Christ. As a result, you may lead someone to Christ, save a marriage, a career, a reputation, or someone's sanity. You may have strengthened someone's faith to carry on trusting in the Lord. That's the blessing of being an encourager—bringing light into the dark places.

I encourage you to daisy up and embrace encouragement.

Today, reach out to someone in need and be that source of encouragement and hope.

Who will that be? _____

What will you do?_____

Journal Prompt:

I remember when _____ was a source of encour-agement to me by…

Prayer:

Heavenly Father, as I look back on my life, you have always been there encouraging and strengthening me. I thank you for the many times you sent someone my way as a source of encouragement. Today let me come alongside someone else as an encourager. I am confident that you will open up an opportunity for me at the right time and in the right place. I am willing and eager to serve in your Name. I truly want to bring light into someone's darkness and despair. Let your light shine through me today. Amen.

Quote:

"Tis a great confidence in a friend to tell him your faults; greater to tell him his." Benjamin Franklin

Day 7

DAISY UP…EMBRACING VICTORY OVER FEAR

So do not fear, for I am with you.

Isa.41:10

Would you agree that we live in a world largely dominated by fear? We see evidence of this with elaborate security systems in our homes, office, cars, and airports. Yet it is the list of personal fears that reside deep within the human soul that create the greatest conflict and bring on ever-increasing anxiety. FDR said, "*The only thing we need to fear is fear itself.*" To feed our preoccupation with fear, producers come up with television shows such as Fear Factor.

One night, as a teenager, I was walking home alone from an evening church service. There was a car parked at the corner of my street. As I hurried past they began to taunt and chase me as I ran to my house. I remember the terror that plagued my dreams for nights afterwards. The incident didn't keep me from going to church but my brother decided to drive me home after the service. God protected me that night and eventually I gained the victory over my fear.

Are you someone who is bound up in fear, tied up in knots, feeling hopeless and helpless? Remember that God has come to set the captives free. That means you and me and all our loved ones. I'm fully believing that God wants to speak courage into your life. Allow Him to replace your fear with faith. Let's discover some important things about fear.

BIBLICAL KINDS OF FEAR

1. FEAR THAT IS COMMANDED

> *"…and now, Israel, what does the Lord your God require of you, but to fear the Lord your God …and to love him." Dt. 10:12*

This fear is a reverent respect and awe for God and daily obedience to his Word. When you truly fear God and reverence his greatness, power, and majesty, other types of fear lose their terror.

2. FEAR THAT IS FORBIDDEN

This kind of fear is synonymous with dread, alarm, terror, apprehension, anxiety and distrust. Webster defines fear as: sudden attack; anxiety caused by real or possible danger; awe; reverence; apprehension or concern; to be afraid; or to expect with misgiving. There's an acrostic that describes fear as:

False

Evidence

Appearing

Real

The devil presents false evidence and makes it seem real. We have a choice to listen to Satan's falsehoods or to believe in our God. The Lord's constant word to us is —fear not. There are actually 366 verses in scripture that tell us to fear not or be not afraid. Fear is the most primitive of all human emotions. All forms of anxiety disorder are rooted in fear. Fear is fear! USA TODAY ran a cover story about what Americans fear and the number one fear was public speaking. That was true for me when I presented my first college speech. I had sweaty palms, knocking knees, and shaky hands. Everyone in that room knew I was nervous and afraid, but they encouraged me, knowing their time was still coming.

CAUSES OF FEAR

Dr. Paul Tournier says, *"Fear creates what it fears."* For example, the skier falls as soon as he begins to be afraid of falling. Circle your causes of fear:

darkness	illness	public speaking	snakes
monsters	violence	changing jobs	spiders
darkness	rape	roller coasters	mice
ghosts	change	being alone	water
bullies	dying	rejection	flying
mistakes	failure	war	disapproval
accidents	aging	terrorism	disasters
bankruptcy	crowds	secrets	truth

As you think about those fears, read the scripture below as a way to claim victory over those fears.

"Fear not, for I have redeemed you; I have called you by your name; you are mine. When you pass through the water, I will be with you. When you walk

through the fire, you shall not be harmed. Nor shall
the flame scorch you." Isa.43:1-2

SYMPTOMS OF FEAR

Do these symptoms sound familiar?

- Your heart begins to race.
- Your breathing becomes shallow and rapid.
- You mouth gets dry.
- Your hands and feet become cold.
- You start to sweat.
- You get the runs.
- Your knees knock and your hands shake.
- Your voice is unsteady.

Check those that apply to you. With these symptoms, you either become ready to fight the object of your fear or decide to run and hide.

STRONGHOLDS

Fear is a serious stronghold. A stronghold is something that takes a "strong hold on you." It can exalt itself in our minds pretending to be bigger or more powerful than our God. It steals much of our focus and causes us to feel overpowered, controlled, and manipulated. Whether the stronghold is an addiction, an unforgiving spirit, despair, depression, anger or fear, it is something that consumes much of our emotional and mental energy. It chokes the life of the Spirit within us. Therefore, we do not fulfill the calling and plan God has for our lives. These are the tactics of the enemy. But we need to remember that the battlefield is in the mind. Our goal is to steal back our thought life and take it captive to Christ.

"We take captive every thought to make it obedient to Christ." 2 Co.10:5

Satan's chief target is the MIND because the most effective way to influence behavior is to influence our thinking. We will act the way we think. Praying scripture verses out loud is a very effective way to change our thinking. Let's keep in mind that absolutely nothing is bigger or more powerful than our God.

Downsize anything that has a hold on you until you have commanded it to bend the knee to the authority of Christ.

FAITH

The opposite of fear is faith. We usually interpret the circumstances of our lives through one or the other. Fear causes us to live emotionally paralyzed. We fear not having enough, so we don't tithe. We fear being hurt, so we withhold love. We fear being taken advantage of, so we don't serve or volunteer. We fear rejection, so we don't step out and do what God has called us to do. Christ comes to you and me and helps us deal with our fear through his power and authority. He does not leave us helpless. Sometimes he rides out the storm with us and other times he calms the storms around us. Most of all, he calms the storms inside us and when he does, we begin to face all the fears that disturb us. They won't paralyze us anymore. They will energize us. God is greater than any fear you will ever face. We have a choice to be a victim and listen to Satan or to be a victor and listen to God. In the Bible we read many stories of God calling his people to some mission outside their comfort zone. In each situation, the person chose how to respond. Were they going to be a victim or victor? Look at the examples below.

Abraham—one of his greatest fears was the unknown. God told him to pack his bags and all his belongings and move to a new place.

Moses—imagine leading the Israelites out of bondage in Egypt at the age of 80. I guess age is no excuse when God tells us to do something.

Gideon—he who considered himself weak, defeated a huge Midianite army with only three hundred warriors.

Esther—she risked her own life to plead the cause of her people with the king.

Jehosophat—God told him not to fear the vast army coming against him because God would fight the battle.

Peter—Jesus told him not to be afraid to walk to him on the water.

The Lord is passing by. He's inviting you to take a risk and step out on the water. Of course you're scared to death. The boat you're in is safe, snug and secure. The water is turbulent, the waves are high, and the wind is severe. If you get out of the boat, you'll sink for sure, but if you don't get out of the boat, you'll never walk on the water. You will eventually die of boredom or stagnation. You will miss your blessing and that would be such a loss. It will be given to someone else even though it was meant for you. What is your boat? Your boat is whatever represents safety and security to you apart from God himself. Whatever keeps you so sheltered and protected that you don't want to give it up. Whatever pulls you away from serving those in need. If you want to know what your boat is, your fear will tell you. In what area of your life are you shrinking back from fully and courageously trusting God? What is it that produces the most fear in you? What will you do if God asks you to confront your fears? Will you walk on the water or stay on the boat? Remember, Jesus is on the water. Peter's getting out of the boat was his gift to the Lord. Peter's walking on the water was Jesus' gift to Peter.

HOW DO WE OVERCOME FEAR?

- Identify and name your fear or stronghold.
- Commit yourself to trust the Lord completely.
- Find scriptures that will give you courage in the face of fear.

Fears are strongholds that can't be swept away with a broom or fly swatter. We can't fuss at them and wish they would flee. Strongholds are broken only one way. They have to be demolished. We have two sticks of dynamite to blast them away: Prayer and the Word of God. These are your weapons of warfare.

It is never the will of God for warfare to become our focus. The fastest way to lose our balance in warfare is to rebuke the devil more than we invoke God. Keep your focus on God believing He is greater and with Him your victory is certain.

Praying scripture creates intimacy with God and renews and retrains the mind. With God on your side, you are an overcomer. The enemy is the defeated foe. We are victorious in Christ.

> *"In all these things, we are more than conquerors through Him who loved us." Ro.8:37*

Today you can be set free from your biggest fear if you proclaim your faith in Christ. Bring it to him in prayer and watch him work magic in your life.

Daisy up Exercises:

What is your greatest fear?

What are the symptoms you experience in fear?

Circle your ordinary response.
Stay and fight   or   Quit and run

How has that worked out for you?

Try these:

- Take several deep breaths and exhale slowly.
- Acknowledge your fear but refuse to allow it to master you.
- Believe that God will deliver you from your fear if you face it with faith.
- Write 5 scriptures about fear that will help you stand firm. Here are some to start with:

  Ps.91:5

  Isa.41:10

  Ps.34:4

  1Jn.4:18

  Ps. 27:1

  2 Tim.1:7

If you like to read, I'd suggest the book: *Feel the Fear and Do It Anyway, Susan Jeffers and Get Out of the Boat, John Ortberg*

Journal Prompt:

The next time I come face to face with my fear, I will…
Draw a picture of your fear and give it a name!

Prayer:

Heavenly Father, I know you have not given me a spirit of fear, but of power, love, and a sound mind. Help me to turn to you for courage and strength when facing fear in my life. Give me faith that will rule over fear. Help me to be secure in you and to trust your unfailing love. With you on my side I have nothing to fear. Without you I have everything to fear. I choose YOU—my all-powerful God! Amen.

Quote:

"Fear defeats more people than any other one thing in the world."
Ralph Waldo Emerson

Day 8

DAISY UP…EMBRACING LIFE

I am the resurrection and the life."

John 11:25

Some time ago, I read an article about Janet Stuart—a young girl from England. Janet's mother had died and she missed her terribly. One day she read the story of the raising of Lazarus in the Bible. It intrigued her and she decided that if it worked for Jesus, it should work for her also. The next day, she marched out to her mother's grave in the back yard and with all her might called out, "Mother, come forth." Nothing happened, so she tried again and then again. She was deeply disturbed and later admitted it caused her young faith to falter. She felt that if she truly believed, then her mother would come back to life. If that's only what it took, then many of us would be standing at gravesides all over this world. But those of us who believe, have the assurance of seeing our loved ones again in heaven. If you have a Bible, take a few moments to read John 11:1-44. This is the story of the raising of Lazarus.

My husband Kenny was in his last days of ALS—Lou Gehrig's disease, when a respiratory illness took hold of him. Now I knew that Jesus loved him and I called on the Lord for help. *"Lord, the one you love is sick." John 11:3* I waited and prayed for a miracle, just like Mary and Martha. But my Kenny went home to God and I was grieving. How I longed for Jesus to miraculously heal him. But I also trusted God's will and his perfect timing for each of our days.

"All the days ordained for me were written in your book
before one of them came to be." Ps.139:16
"Then I called on the name of the Lord." Ps.116:4

How many times have you called on the Lord? What can we learn through times of testing and grief?

- He is the God of all comfort.
- We must wait upon the Lord.
- When we cry out to him, sometimes his answer is yes.
- When we cry out to him, sometimes his answer is no.
- When we cry out to him, sometimes his answer is not now.

- God has a perfect plan for our life.
- His timing is never wrong.
- We need to persevere in prayer.
- We stand on the mountain top and give our complaint to the Lord.

Have you found yourself questioning WHY? At times, the storms of life can pommel against us, leading us to question God's love for us.

In v.21 Martha said, *"Lord, if you had been here, my brother would not have died."*

In v.32 Mary said, *"Lord, if you had been here, my brother would not have died."*

What would you say? Lord, if you had been here, my _____*would not have died.*

WHAT CAN WE LEARN FROM OUR SUFFERINGS AND TRIALS?

- Sometimes we suffer as a consequence of wrong choices.
- Sometimes we suffer to develop our character.

"But we also rejoice in our sufferings, because we know
 that suffering produces perseverance; perseverance,

character; and character, hope.
And hope does not disappoint." Ro.5:3

- Sometimes it's to strengthen our faith.
- Sometimes it's for pruning our character.
- Sometimes it's to glorify God.
- Sometimes it's to bring something out of us that we didn't even know we had. Something we never thought we could handle.

"My grace is sufficient for you, for my power is
made perfect in weakness." 2Cor.12:9
"This sickness will not end in death. No, it is for
God's glory." John 11:4

His friends waited four days and Lazarus died. He was put in the tomb. There was blackness, despair, loneliness, disappointment and grief for Mary and Martha and his friends. John 11:33 tells us that Jesus was deeply moved by their grief. That's because Jesus cares about our suffering. He sees our tears and weeps with us. Jesus wept also. Many of us have had a tomb experience at one time or another. We feel dead and lifeless, just going through the motions. But there is hope for all of us. In v.35 Jesus says, *"I am the resurrection and the life."*

Do you want to live? Will you choose life? Jesus shows us how:

#1 REMOVE THE STONE

"Remove the stone." John 11:39

Martha was worried because it had been four days since Lazarus died but for Jesus it is never too late. With him all things are possible. The stone was the one thing that stood between Lazarus and Jesus.

Are there stones in your life that need to be removed? Are there stones that stand between you and Jesus?

- stone of unforgiveness.
- stone of hidden sin.
- stone of envy and jealousy.
- stone of selfishness.
- stone of self-righteousness.
- stone of pride.
- stone of a judgmental spirit.
- stone of self-pity.
- stone of gossip and slander.
- stone of anger.
- stone of addiction.

- stone of spiritual apathy.
- stone of hopelessness.
- stone of unbelief.
- stone of greed and power.

What is your stone? Would you be willing to write it on the stone?

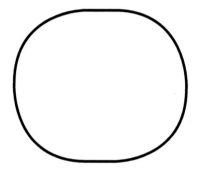

Now pray with believing faith and ask Jesus to remove the stone!

#2 RESPOND

Jesus stood before the tomb and called out, "Lazarus, come forth." John 11:43

His lifeless body became alive again. He obeyed the command. Lazarus didn't wait or hesitate as we often do. We think we know the perfect timing but faith tells us to act now. Is Jesus calling you forth from the tomb? What is keeping you in your tomb?

Check those that apply:

- fear
- self-pity
- perfection
- comfort
- pleasure
- no responsibility

Other:_____

A lot of things happen to us in the tomb and some of them are good. We can learn a lot from our tomb experience and can draw closer to God. But when it's time to come out…COME OUT!

#3 RELEASE

"Take off his grave clothes and let him go." John 11:43

We need to allow others to help us take off our grave clothes. We cannot live in isolation and try to do it all alone. No man is an island. We need each other. There are times we are bound in sin or suffering and we can become too comfortable in those clothes. There are many layers and it takes time to release it all. But that's why we have the body of Christ. Your family and friends will help you get through it so that you can start anew.

"Let us throw off everything that hinders and the sin that so easily entangles and let us run with perseverance the race marked out for us." Heb.12:1

What hinders your walk with God? What entangles you? Throw it off and begin again. With God there are always second chances and more. He wants us to get it right and turn our lives over to Him in complete surrender.

#4 REVEAL

"Therefore many of the Jews who had come to visit Mary, and had seen what Jesus did, put their faith in him."
John 11:45

People are always watching you. They watch how you live, act and speak. They watch how you go through trials and how you treat others. They watch how you pray, love, and serve others. Everyone has a testimony. Don't be afraid to tell others what Jesus has done for you. Your testimony could be a turning point in someone's life.

Let's review:

Remove the stone between you and Jesus.
Respond and obey the command of the Lord.
Release anything that is hindering your walk with Jesus.
Reveal what Jesus has done for you.

> *"I am the Resurrection and the Life" John 11:25*
> *"I am the way, the truth, and the life" John 14:6*

Jesus wants you to have abundant life. He has a purpose for you and wants you to experience joy and contentment. This comes through continuing to develop an intimate relationship with him.

(your name)_____, Come forth. Let Christ shine in you.

Daisy up Exercises:

Visit the graveside of a loved one. Take flowers if you wish. Spend time there, saying whatever you want. Thank them for being part of your life. Tell them you will see them in heaven.

Draw a tombstone: What would you like people to say about you when you are gone? Write an epitaph on the stone.

Visit someone who is isolated, secluded, or lonely. Be a source of joy and encouragement to them.

Journal Prompt:

Today, I choose to come out of my tomb of _____. From now on, I will live….

Prayer:

Heavenly Father, I do not fear death. I long to spend eternity in your Presence. Help me to live with zeal and zest in this life you've given me. I want to enjoy all of your creation and to relish everything as a gift from you. Let me live my life in service of others always speaking words of life into their circumstances. Help me to call forth anyone that is living in a dark tomb of despair or discouragement. You are the way, the truth, and the life. Let me follow you with wholehearted devotion till you call me home. Amen.

Quote:

"To live is the rarest thing in the world. Most people exist, that is all."

Oscar Wilde

Day 9

DAISY UP…EMBRACING PEACE

*"Blessed are the peacemakers, for they
will be called sons of God." Matt. 5:9*

O ne of my favorite movies is *Miss Congeniality* with Sandra
Bullock. She joins the Miss America Contest as an under-
cover FBI agent. The contestants are coached to say they want
"world peace." Isn't that what we all want? Aren't you tired of all
the fighting and violence in the world? In the 1960's there was
the Hippie movement. There were peace signs plastered everywhere, people wore peace shirts, camped out at peace rallies
and sang songs of peace. What do you think of when you hear
the word peace? What images flash before your mind? What
feelings flood your heart?

Have you ever lost your peace? What caused you to lose it?
How did you feel afterwards? Maybe you're reading this today

and wonder where your peace has gone? Is that you? Would you like to have your peace restored? God wants us to have peace in our hearts. In the book of James, it says that we have not because we ask not. Now is the moment to ask God to restore your peace. Before we look at what peace is— let's consider what it is not.

PEACE IS NOT

- The absence of conflict, avoiding, postponing, or putting off important issues. When we do that they only get bigger and more difficult.
- Appeasement, giving in to avoid an argument, or being passive. Jesus was controversial but he stood his ground.
- Keeping the peace at any cost.
- Motivated by fear and distrust.
- False and shallow harmony.

These are the characteristics we find in peacekeepers. These are the people who keep everything behind closes doors. With alcoholics in the family there will be co-dependency issues, denial of the problem, protection of the drinker, and silence about it. With domestic violence the victim becomes a doormat, loses self-esteem, and keeps the peace to avoid abuse.

"Peace, peace when there is no peace." Jer.8:11

"I have no peace, no quietness. I have no rest,
but only turmoil." Job 3:26

"Do not suppose that I have come to bring peace to the earth.
I did not come to bring peace, but a sword." Matt.10:34

What is the meaning of these words? Isn't Jesus called the prince of peace? Didn't he preach about peace? The Jews were expecting a Messiah that would bring an end to Roman rule. They wanted political peace. Jesus didn't come to bring that kind of peace. He came to bring spiritual peace. A peace that would re-establish our relationship with God. Our commitment to Christ will often bring about the opposite of peace. Sometimes the sword will *cut* into families because someone has found faith in Christ. It will *cut* off sinful habits and wrong relationships.

PEACE IS

- Wholeness.
- Completeness.
- Tranquility in the soul.
- Order in place of confusion.
- Authority that is trusted.

"Let the peace of Christ rule in your heart." Col.3:15

A person of peace has a calm demeanor that allows him to conduct himself peacefully even in the midst of difficult and stressful circumstances.

"You will keep in perfect peace him whose mind is steadfast." Isa.26:3

"He himself is our peace." Eph.2:14

God's mark of approval whenever we obey him is peace, that peace which is beyond all understanding. Peace is not having all things in control but knowing and trusting Him who controls all things.

"Seek peace and pursue it." Ps.34:14

This is the role of the peacemaker versus the role of the peacekeeper. A peacemaker is not passive. He is one who is actively overcoming evil with good.

"Do not be overcome by evil, but overcome evil with good." Ro.12:21

A peacemaker finds great satisfaction in diminishing hostilities and bringing about reconciliation between enemies. A peacemaker seeks the truth, settles the issues, and restores relationships to the proper order.

"Make every effort to live in peace with all men." Heb.12:14

HOW TO BE A PEACEMAKER. Let's discover it through an acrostic.

P ROPOSE a peace talk.

"...first go and be reconciled." Matt.5:24

Be the first one to take the initiative to be reconciled. Don't wait for the other person to make the first move. When you meet with them, sit face to face, if that is possible. Realize that conflict is never resolved on its own, it doesn't just go away. Don't postpone, delay, or avoid it. Be a good listener and try to understand the other person's viewpoint. Allow them to speak without interruption or judgment.

E MPATHIZE with their feelings.

"Each of you should look not only to your own interests, but also to the interests of others." Phil.2:4

Have you noticed that when we are upset we're only thinking about ourselves? Hold a peace talk and consider the other person's needs . Empathize with their situation. Ask how you can help. Discover the reason for the other person's hurt and pain.

A DDRESS the problem not the person.

"Do not let any unwholesome talk come out of your mouths." Eph.4:29

Calm your mind before your mouth. Do not criticize or condemn. This will shut them down immediately. Don't compare, assume, or be sarcastic. Above all don't be defensive. That will only build a wall between you.

C OLLABORATE as much as possible.

"Do everything on your part, to live at peace with all men." Ro.12:18

Build a bridge instead of a wall. Pray and go to them in a spirit of love and compromise. It may cost you something, but it will be worth it in the end. Keep in mind that you can't change or fix another person. The only person you can change is yourself. You can change your attitudes and behavior. Extend grace.

E MPHASIZE reconciliation not resolution.

"All this is from God, who reconciled us to himself through Christ and gave us the ministry of reconciliation." 2 Co.5:18

Your goal is to rebuild a relationship. You want to bury the hatchet not the relationship. Agree to disagree. Reconciliation focuses on relationships. Resolution focuses on the problems. Sometimes, reconciliation can help resolve the problems and disagreements. After the Resurrection, Jesus first words to his disciples were about peace.

"Peace I leave with you, my peace I give to you." John 14:27

He is offering that same peace to you today. Let his peace rule…
In your life
In your marriage
In your family
In your relationships

In your workplace

In your finances

In your activities

In your service

In your worship

In your mind and heart

Daisy up today and ask, seek, and work for peace in your own life, in your community, and in the world. Become a peace-maker rather than a peacekeeper.

Daisy up Exercises:

What do you think of when you hear the word peace? What images does it conjure up in your mind? What feelings accompany it? Jot down some of your pictures, words, and feelings in the oval space below:

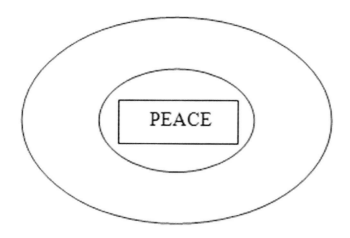

Write down the name of someone you need to make peace with.
Write what you will do to restore peace and when you will do it.
Write a prayer or psalm of peace for that relationship.
Find someone you trust to hold you accountable.

Journal Prompt: To me, peace means… I want peace because…
..I will bring peace into my home and workplace by……….

Prayer:

Heavenly Father, I know that perfect peace resides in you. I thank you for offering me your steadfast peace. There have been times in my life when that peace was broken and shattered because of my own failings. Today, I ask you to restore that peace in my spirit and in my relationships. I promise to do my part also to re-establish peace because of the amazing grace you have shown me. You can make a way even when there seems to be no way. I commit today to walk in a spirit of peace. Amen.

Quote:

"The peace of God is that eternal calm which lies far too deep in the praying and trusting soul to be reached by any external circumstances." A.T. Pierson

Day 10

DAISY UP...EMBRACING PERSEVERANCE

"Let us run with perseverance, the race marked out for us."

Heb.12:1

What does it mean to persevere? When I asked God that question, He answered me with an experience. It happened on an excursion to Kelley's Island with my friend Patti. It was cloudy on the day we started out, but the forecast predicted sun in the afternoon. However, when we arrived at the port, we saw the waves thrashing violently against the rocky shore. It was so rough that only one ferry was running that day. Terrified, we were tempted to turn back and try another day. Instead, we took the challenge and reluctantly boarded the boat. I held on to the bar with white-knuckles, while chanting in my mind, "I'm brave. I'm brave. I'm brave." That afternoon, the sun came out and blessed us with a beautiful day. The ferry ride back later that afternoon was calm and magnificent. I believe that God rewarded our perseverance.

What about you? Have you ever felt like giving up? Ever felt like quitting? Have you ever felt like your situation was so hopeless that your only option was to leave? To just walk away, head out the door, and never come back? Unfortunately, people can do some drastic things when their world starts falling apart and they just can't seem to go on. They make decisions based on feelings and emotions rather than faith. Perhaps some of you are feeling that way today. Are you anxious, overwhelmed and hanging on by a thread? Are you at the end of your rope wanting to call it quits? There are times, however, when we need to quit something in order to go where God wants us to go. But that is not the viewpoint we are discussing today. This is about our journey, our struggles, things out of our control, dreams given us by God, and places where we need to stand firm.

How would it feel if you were given some HOPE today? If you were given some small measure of assurance that you're going to be okay, you're going to make it? You're going to receive all the help you need to

"... run with perseverance, the race marked out for you."
Heb.12:2

What does it mean to persevere? It means to persist, carry on, endure, stand firm, and hang on. Why persevere? We don't do it just for the sake of it, do we? No, we do it because of something or someone we value. They are worth the fight.

I remember the day, in 2003, at our weekly staff meeting when I told everyone about my husband Kenny's diagnosis of ALS—Lou Gehrig's disease. I couldn't stop the flow of tears. Alan Langstaff, a visiting pastor, heard the news earlier in the day. At our weekly prayer meeting that night he preached on Heb.10:23 *"Let us hold unswervingly to the hope we profess, for he who promised is faithful."* He looked straight at us and said, "When you feel you are at the end of your rope, tie a knot and hang on." Those simple words gave both of us immense hope and strength to persevere. That's what I pray for you today—that no one will leave this time with God, discouraged, depressed, or wanting to give up. Be reassured that God's grace is enough for you. God will never quit or walk out on you. He is faithful! So please –don't give up on God! He is able. He will meet you where you are and strengthen you to hang in there.

Today we're going to look at the life of Elijah the Tishbite. His name means THE LORD IS MY GOD. A man of God who also wanted to quit. His story is told in the book of 1 Kings in the Bible. He comes –out of nowhere- a rugged stranger, clothed with camel hair, armed with a zealous heart for God's Word and a faith in the living God. He bursts on the scene with surprising suddenness and dramatic boldness. He was a man of God often called the mightiest of prophets.

But even with great men and women of God, stressful situations can drive them to inappropriate responses. No one is exempt. Let's take a brief look at the life of Elijah the Tishbite. He lived during the reign of Ahab and Jezebel. Ahab did more evil in the sight of God than any of those before him. Jezebel was his wife and had turned him from the worship of Jehovah to the worship of Baal. If this were a fairy tale she would be described as the wicked, evil witch of the north. The northern kingdom was in severe moral and spiritual decline and God sent Elijah to rescue them. In 1Kings 18 he confronted and defeated the prophets of Baal. All 450 of them were killed that day. It was a mighty victory and the people, who had been wavering between Jehovah and Baal, confessed that the Lord was God! But the wicked queen Jezebel immediately got out her iphone and sent him a text threatening to kill him for executing her prophets.

WHAT DID ELIJAH DO?

1Kings 19:3

- "Elijah was afraid and ran for his life."

He knew without a doubt that Jezebel would do what she said. When problems pile up, our first impulse is to run. We leave the conflict for someone else to deal with. We are fearful, extremely tired, feeling rejected, and persecuted.

1Kings 19:4

He came to a broom tree, sat down under it and prayed that he might die. "I've had enough, Lord, he said, "Take my life, I'm no better than my ancestors."

- Elijah was ready to quit….WOE IS ME!!!

Elijah expected things to change for the better. He had visions and dreams of better things to come in Israel. But that wasn't to be. Elijah experienced the depth of fatigue and discouragement just after his two great spiritual victories—the defeat of the Baal prophets and the answered prayer for rain. This happens to all of us from time to time. We may be tempted to quit. You're half way there, hit the wall and want to say ENOUGH. Or you've worked long and hard for a project and it turns out to be a huge success. Then when it's over, there is a let down. You become tired, depressed, and lonely. All you want to do is quit. And this is exactly where Satan wanted Elijah and where he wants you. He wants you to QUIT and not to trust God.

WHAT DID GOD DO?

1 Kings 19:5-8

- God gave him rest and nourishment.

God sees that the journey is too much for Elijah so God sends an angel to him twice to give him food and water and to make sure he gets plenty of rest. If you don't get enough sleep, God will find a way to force you to rest and get replenished.

Ps.62:1-5 "My soul finds rest in God alone."

Elijah then journeyed 40 days and 40 nights to get to Mount Horeb the Mountain of God. When he got there he hid in a cave. God called out to him.

1 Kings 19:9-10 "What are you doing here, Elijah?"

"I've been very zealous for the Lord God Almighty. The Israelites have rejected your covenant, broken down your altars, and put your prophets to death with the sword. I am the only one left, and now they are trying to kill me too."

- God let Elijah vent.

Elijah pours out his feelings and complaints to the Lord. He feels like he doesn't deserve what's happening to him. After all, he's been zealous for the Lord. He probably feels some sense of entitlement and wonders why these things are happening to him after all He's done for Lord. God can handle our feelings and He wants us to be honest with him pouring out our hearts to Him. He hears us and will answer us.

When you want to give up, God reminds you who He is.

1 Kings 19:11 "Go out and stand on the mountain in the presence of the Lord, for the Lord is about to pass by."

God showed demonstrations of power...the wind, earthquake, and fire

But he wasn't in them. He was in the gentle whisper. That's when we hear him best also- in our times of quiet and solitude.

- God gave Elijah a task and some friends

1 Kings 19:15-16, 18

God tells him to get back to work. He gives him a task to go and anoint Hazael king over Aram, Jehu king over Israel, and Elisha to succeed him as prophet. When you are full of self-pity, you need to get your eyes off of yourself and back onto

God and his purpose for your life. If you're breathing, if you're alive, you have a purpose. This is the time you do something for others. All of us, at one time or another, may be tempted to quit. We may feel like we can't go on or persevere another hour or day. At times like this, we need to understand that God is at work in our lives. We don't persevere in our own strength, we persevere by God's grace, in spite of difficulties, obstacles, or discouragement.

"My grace is sufficient for you, for my power is made perfect in weakness." 2Co.12:9

Elijah shows us that even if we slip up or make mistakes, we can pick ourselves up and begin again. He had a momentary melt down, but he got back up and persevered in the work of the Lord. We don't have to do it alone! God told Elijah there were 7000 others who had not worshipped Baal. God also tells us we're not alone, for he has given us family, friends, and mentors to walk this journey with us and to help us persevere.

With FAITH you know that all things are possible with God. Wouldn't it be great if you came before God today and said, "I'm going to do it. I'm going to stand firm. I'm going to keep running the race. I'm not going to quit." That's an empowering proclamation. I pray you have the courage to say it before God.

Daisy up Exercises:

Write your name in the blank below.

WHY ARE YOU HERE, _____?

WHERE DO YOU NEED PERSEVERANCE? Check any below that apply to you.

Are you dealing with a chronic illness?

Are you trying to save your marriage?

Are you waiting for a change in your life?

Are you waiting for a job?

Are you praying for your finances to get better?

Are you working hard for a promotion that never comes?

Are you dealing with difficult things in your home?

Are you caring for elderly or sick parents?

Are you giving up on your dreams, hopes, and desires?

Are you waiting for your soul mate?

Are you praying for your children to make it?

Are you praying for salvation for loved ones?

Are you waiting for an adoption?

Other _____

Go to your Bible concordance and find 3-5 scriptures that will motivate and remind you to persevere in the storms of your life.

Journal Prompt:

Write about where you most need to persevere. What is it? What are the obstacles you are facing? What are you feeling? What steps can you take to persevere? Who will you ask to help you?

Prayer:

Lord, help me to run my race with perseverance. I trust in your love for me and that gives me strength. When I grow tired and weary, help me to fix my eyes on you and on the finish line. Restore my energy and revive my spirit. Help me to endure and persevere. I don't want to be a quitter…I want to be a finisher! Your grace upholds me, Lord. Let me Daisy Up in your strength. Amen.

Quote:

"You may encounter many defeats, but you must not be defeated. In fact, it may be necessary to encounter the defeats, so you can know who you are, what you can rise from, how you can still come out of it." Maya Angelou

Day 11

DAISY UP...EMBRACING A DIFFERENT LIGHT

"The unfolding of your words gives light;
it gives understanding to the simple."
Ps.119:130

We have often heard the Holy Spirit referred to as the Counselor, Comforter, and Guide, but today I want to invite you to look at the Holy Spirit in a different light as a different light. Let's begin with three short stories.

The first is about the purchase of our house on Roosevelt Street. When our realtor, a close friend of ours, showed us the house for the first time, she was aghast. She noticed the horrible carpet, floor to ceiling wallpaper in every room and a strong cat odor. She tried to usher us out of the house as quickly as possible. She wanted the best for us and this wasn't it. I, on the other hand, saw openness, possibility, and potential. I noticed a fireplace, a Florida room out back, solitude, spruce trees, and even a lovely basement. We saw five other houses that day, but that evening I called and told her my favorite house was the one on Roosevelt Street. She started to protest but I asked her to return and look at it with new eyes. She agreed and she too saw it in a different light. Something can look different when we change the way we look at it.

The second story is about my sister Gloria. She began taking art classes having no talent or skill in that area. She was learning about perspective in art but found it very hard to apply. She practiced and practiced drawing things in perspective until she finally "got it." She has become an accomplished artist now but she learned that it takes time and practice to get the perspective just right.

The third story is about a book written by Andy Andrews called *The Noticer.* The story takes place in a quaint little town by the gulf coast. The main character is an older man named Jones, with white hair, crystal blue eyes, and a deeply wrinkled face. He always wore jeans and a tee shirt with flip flops. He appeared out of nowhere and always carried a brown suitcase with him. The book shares his encounters with the homeless, college age students, businessmen who lost their integrity, couples with their marriage in trouble, people in financial difficulty, and widows and the elderly. He began by telling them his name was simply Jones. He helped them to start noticing things, checking the attitude of their hearts, and getting a different perspective. When people asked him who he was, the answer was always the same: *a noticer.* He claimed it was his gift to notice things about people that others might overlook. He noticed things about people and their situation that produced a special perspective, a broader view, that allowed them to refocus, and begin their lives again. Jones was a man of character, wit, perception, and courage. He helped people look at things in a different light.

WHAT IS PERSPECTIVE?

It is a mental view or outlook, a frame of reference, a way of regarding situations, and facts and judging their relational importance. We all have perspective.

We received certain perspectives from our childhood, our culture, and the people we hang out with. Other perspectives come from books we read, media, movies, culture and religious backgrounds. The way we look at something affects the way we feel and the way we act. Perspective is something we have control over and can change. Change can foster two emotions in us: enthusiasm and fear.

Oprah wants you to change.

Dr. Phil wants you to change.

Dr. Oz wants you to change.

Weight Watchers want you to change.

Bookstores offer you 365 daily secrets to change.

Your spouse wants you to change.

Your children want you to change.

Your boss wants you to change.

Your government wants you to change.

Your community wants you to change.

We all buy into it and want to change our clothes, hairstyles, waistline, muscles, job, house, cholesterol, car, ipods, teeth, and relationships.

We also want to change our tempers, our greed, our laziness, our service, our attitude, our habits, our worship, and our devotion.

GOD WANTS US TO CHANGE

He wants to become our number one priority. He wants to have a personal relationship with him. We need to get rid of the idols in our lives that separate us from him.

HOW DO WE CHANGE OUR PERSPECTIVE?

We change it through the power of his Holy Spirit and his revealed Word.

Have you ever changed the way you look at things as a result of reading and praying over God's Word, from hearing the still small voice within, from a Bible study, a small group discussion, a divine appointment, a conference, sermon or retreat? When perspective comes from the Holy Spirit, it is power-packed, dynamic, vibrant, life-giving, fruit-bearing, strengthening, energizing, positive, hopeful, believing, courageous, purposeful, and life-changing. That's the kind of perspective I want in my life. How about you?

"Do not conform any longer to the pattern of this world, but be transformed by the renewing of your mind." Ro.12:2

The Word of God is filled with stories about people and their perspectives.

Let's get a brief overview of a few of these amazing accounts.

Numbers 13-14 Twelve spies were sent by Moses to explore Canaan the promised land. When they returned, ten of them said it would be impossible to conquer, while Joshua and Caleb believed that they could conquer the land with God on their side. The perspective of fear resulted in forty years of wandering in the desert. If the Israelites had opted for the perspective of belief, they would have been victorious in conquering Canaan and moved into the Promised Land.

1 Sam. 17 David and Goliath

Saul and the Israelite army were dismayed and terrified of the giant Goliath. David on the other hand saw God as his giant and therefore killed Goliath with a slingshot and a stone. Saul and his army had a spirit of fear which kept them weak and powerless. David had a spirit of faith and courage and that gave him victory and a promising future.

Matt. 5:43 Jesus's Sermon on the Mount

"Love your neighbor and hate your enemy. But I tell you: Love your enemies and pray for those who persecute you."

There are many other examples in scripture of people changing their perspective and seeing things in a different light. There's a commercial on television that expresses it perfectly. When your eyes are smiling, you're smiling. When they're laughing, you're laughing. Be kind to your eyes with transition lenses. They adapt to changing light. So you see your whole day comfortably and conveniently while protecting your eyes from the sun. Ask your eye care professional which transition lenses are right for you? Might I suggest that you ask the Holy Spirit to be your eye care professional. He will certainly give you the right transition lenses. Take a moment to think about what God might be asking you to see in a different light. Is he asking you to exchange your perspective about something or someone with His perspective? In what areas are you angry, stubborn, resisting, or unmoved? Circle the areas where you need to change your perspective.

A personal relationship.

A circumstance or situation.

A trial or struggle or illness.

An addiction or challenge.

Your past sins.

Your financial situation or job search.

A person you refuse to forgive.

The willingness to use your gifts in the church.

The amount you tithe.

Joining a small group.

Going on a mission trip.

Volunteering to work with the poor.

One of my favorite stories is about a man who told his pastor that he wanted to divorce his wife. He just didn't love her anymore. So the pastor told him to take one month and do all kinds of wonderful things for her. Bring her chocolates and flowers, take her to a resort, enjoy candlelight dinners, take her dancing, and tell her how beautiful she looks. The pastor said he could divorce her after that month. Many months went by before the pastor saw the man again. He asked if he divorced his wife. The man replied, "Are you kidding? I'm married to a goddess." That's what a change in perspective can do for you.

Where do you need to change your perspective? Ask the Holy Spirit to bring that particular thing or person to your mind. Your entire situation or relationship can change if you change your perspective. Let's take a moment to go back to JONES. At the end of the story, he disappears but leaves his suitcase. Everyone was curious to know what was in that suitcase that he guarded so diligently. The townspeople gathered in a little diner and opened the suitcase. I won't tell you what was in it because you may want to read the book. Let me just say that it was loving and meaningful. I hope it raises your curiosity and impels you to check out *The Noticer* by Andy Andrews.

Can you imagine the impact we could make on this world, if we allowed the Holy Spirit to change our perspectives according to God's way? Then imagine what would happen if we helped others to change their perspective according to God's way. We would be helping people live fuller, happier, and more productive lives.

Let's ask the Holy Spirit to help us plant his seeds of new perspective in our own situations. We do it one small step at a time, one day at a time, one person at a time. It brings great joy to see things in a different light!

For God who said, "Let light shine out of darkness" made his light shine in our hearts to give us the light of the knowledge of the glory of God in the face of Christ. 2Co.4:6

Daisy up Exercises:

Get a large piece of newsprint. Fold it in half. At the top of the left column write —

My Perspective—at the top of the right column write God's Perspective. Then write a list of things that you are struggling with under the left column. After each one, write your honest perspective about it. In the right column write how you can change your perspective about it according to God's counsel. This exercise can bring a whole new light on your relationships and circumstances.

Journal Prompt: All of a sudden, her perspective about____
_____changed because of_____
_____…

Prayer:

Heavenly Father, sometimes I get obsessed with my own point of view and refuse to see things differently. Open my heart and my mind to hear from your Holy Spirit. Allow me to not only listen to the opinions of others but to actively seek them out. Give me a humble and willing spirit to see people and circumstances differently. Give me grace to change my perspective to your perspective. I yearn for your light and your truth in my life. Amen.

Quote:

"What we see depends mainly on what we look for." John Lubbock

Day 12

DAISY UP.......EMBRACING EXPECTATION

"Silver and gold I do not have, but what I have I give you-
In the "name of Jesus of Nazareth, walk."
Acts 3:6

O ur story today begins in the book of Acts. I'd like to invite you to take a moment to quiet yourself in God's presence and ask His Holy Spirit to bring fresh revelation during your time in his Word today. Now reverently open your bible and slowly read Acts 3:1-10

Let's look at these verses individually.

v.1 "One day Peter and John were going up to the temple
at the time of prayer- at three in the afternoon."

The Jews observed three times of prayer a day: 9:00 a.m., 3:00 p.m., and sunset. Notice that Peter and John were going to the temple. There is power and blessing in the house of God when believers come together. If they hadn't gone to the temple that day a powerful miracle and testimony would not have occurred. It is heart breaking that many Christians today neglect the simple act of attending church regularly. They miss out on the spirit of joy, love, and encouragement that occurs when people come together in faith. Jesus taught the apostles and disciples the importance of solitary prayer as well as corporate worship.

What are your thoughts and feelings about attending church? Was it part of your upbringing? Is it something you do as a family? Is it something you'd like to do?

_____

_____

v.2 "A man crippled from birth was being carried to the Temple Gate called Beautiful where he was put every day to beg from those going into the temple courts."

This gate called beautiful was an impressive sight. Much of it was made from Corinthian bronze and inlaid with ornately decorated gold. It's dazzling brightness could be seen from quite a distance. It was one of the nine gates that led through a section known as the middle wall of partition. Gentiles and Jews who were physically deformed in any way were not allowed beyond this point by penalty of death. They were never allowed into the temple area, yet sitting under this magnificent structure was a suffering human being. In our own day, who might be refused entrance to a church because of their appearance, dress, color, or behavior?

This man was crippled, unable to walk, dependent on others, paralyzed and incapacitated. For every person crippled physically there are thousands crippled spiritually. Crippled because they....

- Do not have a relationship with Jesus.
- Are bound by a spirit of depression or discouragement.
- Wracked with worry and anxiety and stress.
- Chained by addiction to drugs, alcohol, or porn.
- Held captive by a spirit of bitterness and unforgiveness.
- Suffering from a broken heart caused by rejection, abuse, or betrayal.
- Fighting circumstances that are beyond their control.
- Their marriage and family is breaking apart.
- Constantly deal with issues of shame or low self-esteem.

Whatever it is—sit at the Gate called Beautiful and hold your sign:

What does your sign say?

Many people passed through this gate on their way to worship. This man was begging where he would be seen by the most people. Giving money to beggars was considered praiseworthy in the Jewish religion. How do you feel when you pass a beggar on the street or see someone holding a sign that says "Will work for food?" Do you feel it is praiseworthy to help them out or do you avoid eye contact and walk on? What is your normal reaction? Jot down some of your thoughts in the space below.

What about you? Are you holding a sign hoping to receive something from God today? Here are a few steps for receiving from God.

#1. ASK

v.3 "When he saw Peter and John about to enter,
he asked them for money."

The key word here is *asked*. The beggar asked for money because he thought that was what he needed. How often do we think money is the answer to all our needs? How often do we say, *Show me the money*. But God has something much better for us. When this poor beggar called out for help, Peter and John heard him and responded. Do you listen for the cries of beggars in your life? Sometimes they are right in front of you but you do not see or hear them. Ask the Lord to open your eyes to see and your ears to hear the cries of the poor.

#2. LOOK

v.4 " Peter looked straight at him, as did John.
Then Peter said, 'Look at us.'"

Peter and John looked straight at the beggar and told him to look at them. As the beggar did so, his faith was quickened by God's word. Where do you look when you are crippled? Do you call or text your friends, reach out for self-help books, eat ice cream, demand your own way, or turn to God? Where are you looking? Are you looking in all the wrong places? God is telling us to look at Him. He looks at you with eyes of love and compassion. He wants the best for your life.

#3 EXPECT

v.5 "So the man gave them his attention, expecting
to get something from them."

Expect means to anticipate, hope for, want, desire, or look forward to. Of course, this man was expecting money. What about you? What do you expect from God?

- Love
- Deliverance
- Victory over sin
- Healing
- Wealth
- Spiritual gifts
- Marriage and children
- Possessions

How many times do we pray without expecting? We ask but we don't believe. We limit God by our own small thinking, don't we? Often we expect God to do things in a certain way and at a specific time. But God will always do it His way. His ways are not our ways.

v.6 Then Peter said, "Silver and gold I do not have, but what I have I give you. In the name of Jesus of Nazareth, walk."

Peter was inviting this man to exercise his faith in Jesus of Nazareth to be healed. Peter never flinched, hesitated, or doubted that this man would be healed. That's because he was filled with the power of the Holy Spirit. We too have that power of the Holy Spirit to touch and heal others' lives.

v.7 "Taking him by the right hand, he helped him up, and instantly the man's feet and ankles became strong."

When you expect God to do something, his power immediately begins to operate. Faith is the switch that turns on or releases the power of God. Faith is not in the head, it is in the heart.

"For it is with your heart that you believe and are justified."
Ro.10:10

Faith is a gift from God and to each is given a specific measure. We can't earn it but we can sincerely ask God to increase our faith and He will honor our prayer.

#4. BELIEVE AND ACT IN FAITH

v.8 "He jumped to his feet and began to walk."

There were no excuses. He had faith to listen to Peter's commands and to act on them. If he just continued to sit there, nothing would have happened. God will never force us to believe. He asks us to believe and receive. Today can be an *instantly* for you if you will believe and act in faith. Take a step of faith!

#5. GIVE GOD THE PRAISE

v.8 "Then he went with them into the temple courts, walking and jumping, and praising God."

He was filled with JOY! This beggar was crippled and now he could walk and even jump. He couldn't help but give praise to God. That delights the heart of God when we praise and thank him for what he does for us. We don't want to be like the 9 lepers who did not return to give thanks.

#6 TESTIFY

v.9 "When all the people saw him walking and praising God, they recognized him as the same man who used to sit begging at the gate called Beautiful and they were filled with wonder and amazement at what had happened to him."

People were filled with amazement because they witnessed a miracle that was done in the name of Jesus. Now they were prepared to listen to Peter's words about Jesus of Nazareth. Have you ever noticed how your faith grows when you see a miracle or hear of someone's testimony of salvation or healing? That's why we should never hesitate to share our testimony with others. Give it to a friend, small group, or large group as an act of praise and thanksgiving.

Daisy up Exercises:

WHAT DO YOU NEED JESUS OF NAZARETH TO DO FOR YOU TODAY?

Read these slowly and reverently as an act of faith in God.

Place a check mark in front of all that might apply to you personally.

- Today in the name of Jesus of Nazareth, you can be healed from anything that is crippling you. Receive it in faith.
- Today in the name of Jesus of Nazareth, you can let go of your past and receive healing...physical, spiritual and emotional. Receive.
- Today in the name of Jesus of Nazareth, you can be delivered from addiction to drugs or alcohol or anything that has power over you.
- Today in the name of Jesus of Nazareth, your marriage can be restored.
- Today in the name of Jesus of Nazareth, you can be released of bitterness, anger and resentment.
- Today in the name of Jesus of Nazareth, you can be filled with the Holy Spirit.
- Today in the name of Jesus of Nazareth, you can be cleansed of all your sins.
- Today in the name of Jesus of Nazareth, you can be set free from depression and discouragement.
- Today in the name of Jesus of Nazareth, you can find it in your heart to forgive someone who has hurt you.

You can begin to expect your life to change and be transformed, if you sit at the gate called Beautiful and Ask, Look, Expect, Believe, and Receive.

Journal Prompt:

Imagine you are the one sitting at the gate called Beautiful... where are you crippled? Ask Jesus to heal you ...what changes would that make in your life? How would you feel? Write freely and honestly for at least 20 minutes.

Prayer:

Heavenly Father, I come before you today in a posture of expectation. I'm asking in a spirit of faith, that I will be _____. Thank you that I can look to you to fulfill all my needs and my deepest desires. I want to embrace the hope of expectation in my life as I start this new day. Thank you for your Word today and for your grace to step out into a new day. I ask for all that I need today in the name of Jesus of Nazareth.

Quote:

"Today, expect something good to happen to you no matter what occurred yesterday. Realize the past no longer holds you captive. It can only continue to hurt you if you hold on to it. Let the past go. A simply abundant world awaits." Sarah Breathnach

Day 13

DAISY UP…EMBRACING THE GREEN-EYED MONSTER

"Love does not envy." 1 Co.13:4

*T*oday I want to talk about something that many people consider a trivial thing. It rears its ugly head and it's name is ENVY. I want to put it on a series of billboards and expose it for what it really is—a green-eyed monster! He's dark and sinister, sitting on a throne, hidden in the closet of our hearts under lock and key. We never want him exposed to the light.

To be perfectly honest, all of us have at one time or another been envious of others. Although we all struggle with envy it's hard to admit it. Why? Because it's an ugly emotion and it causes us to feel shame. But we will never be able to dethrone this monster unless we embrace him and bring him out of our closets and into the light. He is an insidious destroyer.

"A heart at peace gives life to the body, but envy rots the bones." Prov.14:30

Envy is dangerous to the soul because it doesn't leave quickly. We fixate on it as we ruminate and brood over it. Envy is universal but when left unchecked it can ruin your life. It is a grim and malicious sin and can make you do evil things.

According to an ancient Greek legend, a certain athlete ran well but placed second in the race. The winner was acclaimed with much praise, and eventually a statue was erected in his honor. Envy ate away at the man who came in second. He resented the winner so much that he became obsessed with the idea of demolishing the statue. Every night he went to the statue under cover of darkness, chiseling away at the base to debilitate the foundation. But one night his dark anger went too far and the heavy marble statue crashed down on him. He died beneath the weight of the marble replica of the man he had grown to hate. His own envy had flattened and destroyed him.

BILLBOARD #1   WHAT ENVY IS

Let's clarify the difference between jealousy and envy. Jealousy is fear that you will lose something valuable. It is a proud possession of something that we are unwilling to share with another. It can be the source of sadness when your friend prefers another over you. But envy is the anger you feel because someone else got what you wanted. It can bring you despondency when another is praised instead of you. Envy is sadness, displeasure, bitterness or a hostile feeling toward someone because that person has something that we want- but do not have- and we want to steal it from them. We think we deserve it more. The truth is that envy is the sin of the "have nots" against the "haves." And to acknowledge that we're envious is to admit that we feel inadequate. Envy doesn't mean you can't have a goal, dream, or desire. It doesn't mean that you can't admire someone else's gifts. Envy resents somebody who already has what you desire and you are not grateful for what you do have. For example, when I was in the first grade, I was envious of my friend because she had a jump rope and I didn't. And in high school, I was envious of another friend when she got honored for a title and contest that I wanted to win. Ouch. Just thinking about it makes me feel shallow and ashamed. Other examples of envy might be:

talents	beauty
spiritual gifts	a body to die for
success	character
popularity	friends
wealth	family
career	fame

position	promotion
status	home
possessions	opportunities

Envy is based on the myth: "I have to have more to be happy." Envy always looks at others and asks: "Why them? Why not me? Don't I deserve it too?"

Erma Bombeck said, "Lord, if you cannot make me thin, at least make my friends look fat." No matter how blessed we've been our natural tendency is to want the blessing we do not have.

BILLBOARD #2   WHO ENVY AFFECTS

Mirror, mirror, on the wall, who's the fairest of them all?

We are all affected in some way by the sin of envy. It is especially the sin of the successful. The higher a man ascends, the more prone he is to envy.

BIBLICAL EXAMPLES

Gen. 4   Envy caused Cain to kill his brother Abel.

Gen.26:14   The Philistines envied Isaac because he owned many flocks, herds, and servants leading them to plug up his wells.

Gen.30	Rachael envied Leah because she was barren and Leah was the mother of many children.
Gen.37	Joseph's brothers sold him into slavery because of envy.
1 Sam.18	Saul was envious of David and tried to kill him many times.
Daniel	Satraps were envious of Daniel, his gifts and his position, so they set a trap for him which led to their own deaths.
Matt.27	It was out of envy that the Jewish leaders had Jesus arrested and crucified.

The closer a person is to you the greater your envy is likely to be. We don't have problems with people thousands of miles away. It's the people next door, in your own family, workplace, or church that cause division, dissensions, bitterness, and jealousy.

"For where you have envy and selfish ambition, there you find disorder and every evil practice." James 3:16

Preachers can become envious of large mega churches, more baptisms, better preaching, outreach causes that are highlighted in the news and media. It's clear that envy is the most common destroyer of family and friendships. It resents

God's goodness to others and ignores God's goodness to me. Our real struggle is not with the person we envy, it's with God. We're saying, "Lord, you made a mistake when you gave that person so many blessings. I deserve some of what you gave him/her."

BILLBOARD #3   SIGNS OF ENVY

- We secretly regret our friends have succeeded.
- We believe we would have done a much better job.
- We use excuses to explain why someone else received the honor.
- We temper our compliments with "but".
- We complain others don't appreciate us as they should.
- We walk the other way rather than compliment someone.
- We question the motives of those who show kindness to us.
- We secretly gloat when someone else gets caught or exposed.
- We can't sincerely rejoice with others on their personal success.
- We can't bear to hear our friends complimented in our presence.
- We say "I really like so and so but I want to make sure you have all the facts."

- We're better at criticism than praise.
- We drag others down to lift ourselves higher.

BILLBOARD #4   WHAT ENVY DOES

- Keeps our relationships from growing.
- Judges other people's motives.
- Reveals the sorry condition of our heart.
- Is sinful and has weighty consequences.
- Leads to worry and anxiety in our lives.
- Diminishes the joy in our own life.
- Disregards God's Word.
- Makes us self-absorbed and self-centered.
- Traps us in making comparisons.
- Compels us to be ungrateful for our blessings.
- Disposes us to a lack of trust in God.

A NEW BILLBOARD CAMPAIGN: THREE WAYS TO OVERCOME ENVY

BILLBOARD #1 CHANGE YOUR MIND

"To be made new in the attitude of your mind." Eph.4:23
"Do not conform any longer to the pattern of this world, but be transformed by the renewing of your mind." Ro.12:2

Admit it.

Confess it.

Agree with God that envy is wrong and ask him to remove it from your life.

BILLBOARD #2 CHANGE YOUR HEART AND PUT ON LOVE

"Love does not envy." 1 Co.13:4

"A new command I give you: Love one another." John 13:34

"Love must be sincere. Hate what is evil; cling to what is good. Be devoted to one another in brotherly love." Ro.12:9-10

"For Christ's love compels us." 2Co.5:14

"…and let us consider how we may spur one another on toward love and good deeds." Heb.10:24

BILLBOARD #3 CHANGE YOUR DIRECTION

ACCEPT *"Accept one another then, just as Christ accepted you."* Ro.15:7

BEAR *"Be completely humble and gentle; be patient, bearing with one another in love."* Eph.4:2

SERVE   *"Serve one another in love." Gal.5:13*

PRAY   *"Pray for those who persecute you." Matt.3:44*

                        "Pray for each other that you may be healed."

                        Jas.5:16

The effects of our envy can be far-reaching and the consequences can touch and change the lives of those we love. Overcoming envy is a day by day, hour by hour, minute by minute challenge. Don't get discouraged. Acknowledge it for what it is and then change your thoughts and feelings.

"Do not be overcome by evil, but overcome evil with good."
Ro.12:21

WE ARE OVERCOMERS IN CHRIST!

Daisy up Exercises:

Write the name of someone you envy on the sign below:

Now list the things you are envious of:

Next ask God to take away your envy.

Write a prayer that God will continue to bless and show favor to that person you envy.

When you have an opportunity, praise and compliment that person in sincerity.

Journal Prompt:

Write a Dear God letter thanking Him for all the ways He has blessed you…be specific in listing all of them.

Prayer:

Heavenly Father, thank you for the many favors and blessings you have showered on me. Please forgive me for envying what you have chosen to give to others. Release me from a spirit of envy or jealousy and help me to be grateful for what you have given me. Help me to freely praise the gifts in others. Keep my eyes focused on you…my true treasure. I am the richest person alive because I have this awesome relationship with you. May I use the gifts you have given me to bless those less fortunate. I pray this in Jesus name. Amen.

Quote:

"Love looks through a telescope; envy through a microscope."
Josh Billings

Day 14

DAISY UP... EMBRACING YOUR GIANTS

"Be strong and courageous." Josh.3:9

*W*ouldn't it be wonderful to know you had the power to overcome the giants in your life? Well, guess what? You do have that power in the name of the living God. I'm praying that by the end of today's reflection, you'll stand up and say— Yes, I'm a **GO—Giant Overcomer** and I will find the courage to face and overcome at least one of my fears.

If you are going to face a giant, you need to know what a giant is. Remember the movie Jurassic Park? Those dinosaurs were enormous giants. In general terms, a giant is someone or something that is colossal, huge, immense, mammoth, and enormous. And let's also consider the meaning of the word *overcome*. It means to gain a superior position over; to conquer.

So if we put these two thoughts together it means to gain the power and victory over something much bigger than you. That empowering thought can lead to an empowering action.

Are you ready to overcome some giants today? Are you sitting back in a recliner just nodding your head or are you sitting upright...expectant and eager to see what God is speaking to you this morning? I'm a person who loves labels and if you happen to have one in a drawer, take it out and write GO on it and then stick it on your hand, your forehead , or your shirt. If you don't have any labels, just write it on a piece of paper and keep it before you.

"I have given you authority to trample on snakes and scorpions and to <u>overcome </u>all the power of the enemy." Lk 10:19

In our reflection today, we will see how the Israelites came face to face with a Giant. Open your Bible to 1Sam.17:1. Many of you are familiar with the story of David and Goliath. In our modern day we might call it David and the Terminator. Let's ask God to give us fresh insights as He lays this story before us. The Israelites are at war with the Philistines. The Philistines, their arch enemies, occupied one hill and the Israelites another, with the valley of Elah between them. A champion named Goliath, who was from Gath, came out of the Philistine camp. Here is what the Israelites saw:

- A man who was an enormous giant.
- A man over nine feet tall.
- A man with a bronze helmet.
- A man with a coat of armor of bronze weight 5000 shekels (125 lbs).
- A man with bronze on his legs.
- A man holding a spear shaft and iron point 600 shekels.
- A man with a shield bearer before him.

You can understand why the Israelites were terrified. The Giant positions himself and bellows a challenge to the Israelites. He dares them to send a man to come and fight him. If this man killed him then the Philistines would become their subject. But if the giant won, the Israelites would become subjects of the Philistines. Every day for forty days, morning and evening, Goliath hollered the same challenge. He defied the ranks of Israel. It's obvious that Goliath was feeling arrogant, unafraid and overly confident. But Saul and his army were dismayed and terrified. They didn't know what to do.

Israel had a problem and it's name was **FEAR**—meaning dread, apprehension, anxiety, alarm, fright, terror, and trepidation. Israel was hiding in sheer terror. We are all too familiar with these emotions aren't we? People all over the world are riddled with fears and phobias. Fear is so real and relevant that God has over 400 verses in the Bible relating to fear.

"Be strong and courageous; do not be terrified; do not be discouraged, for the Lord your God will be with you wherever you go." Joshua 3:9

Saul was supposedly the natural challenger for Goliath. He was a Benjamite and the biggest man in the kingdom. *1Sam.9:2* describes him as an impressive young man without equal among the Israelites, a head taller than any of the others. So what did Saul do? He and his people hid in their tents hoping day after day that Goliath would disappear. But unfortunately, the giant stayed at his post day after day, mocking, taunting, and ridiculing the Israelite army.

Let's examine 4 principles for overcoming your Giant.

Principle #1 Name and Face Your Giant

Ask yourself what is taunting, tempting, or mocking you in your life. It's something that's always with you. It's there when you go to bed and when you awake. It's like a pesky mosquito always buzzing around your ear. Circle any below that might apply to you:

fear   alcohol   infidelity   greed

pride   materialism   peer pressure   gluttony

lust	bitterness	finances	depression
guilt	shame	abuse	disease
envy	jealousy	dishonesty	rebellion
drugs	past sins	unforgiveness	lying

- Identify your Giant…every giant has a name.
- Identify what it is doing to you and possibly your family.

David enters the scene. He is the youngest of Jesse's eight sons. His 3 oldest brothers are fighting in Saul's army. His father sent him with food for his brothers and their commander. He reached camp as the army was going out to its battle positions, while Goliath was shouting his defiance of the army of Israel. This only increased the Israelites' fear.

Principle #2 Be Prepared For Giant Appearances

Giants don't just suddenly show up. Their appearance is well timed. When they do show up, we tend to get discouraged, defeated, and depressed. But we have to understand that nothing comes our way apart from the will of God. If we believe this it would change our attitudes toward our giants. Now at this point, David's anger is roused and he asks, *"Who is this uncircumcised Philistine that he should defy the armies of the Living God?" 1Sam.17:26.* David had a cause- He was a man after God's own heart. Then David's words were overheard and reported to Saul. David offers to kill the giant but Saul says he is not able since he is only a boy. David boasts that he has killed lions and bears to protect his sheep. He says the Philistine is just like one of them because he defied the armies of the living God. Eventually, Saul agrees to let David try to kill the Giant. David is uncomfortable in Saul's armor and takes it off. We also cannot fight in someone else's armor. We need to rely on our own proven weapons of prayer and the Word of God.

Principle #3 Listen to God, not to Your Detractors

David refused to listen to his oldest brother's anger. He listened to God instead.

We too need to listen to God and turn off the voices of those who are envious, jealous, or unbelieving. There will be people who try to thwart our plans instead of supporting us.

"I come against you in the name of the Lord Almighty- the God of the Armies of Israel whom you have defied. This day the Lord will hand you over to me and I'll strike you down and cut off your head." 1 Sam.17:45

Principle #4 Slay Your Giant/ Finish the Fight

One thing we learn from David is to be certain you don't just stun your giant. Kill your giant. If you don't, the giant will wake up and come at you again. Every giant you kill is a victory God gives you and it prepares you to face and defeat the next giant that comes into your life. Think about this: Goliath wasn't the Giant. David was the Giant because of his great faith in God.

Looking at your life in the present, what Giants are you facing? Your greatest Giant is anything that stands between you and doing what God has called you to do. Giants don't fall easily, they don't just go away. They will eventually consume and destroy you. They are not just a figment of your imagination, they are real. And the only way we will defeat our giants is to get a good look at the size and power of our God. Would you like to see your giant defeated today? Believe God and He will deliver that Giant into your hands and you will be a **GO…Giant Overccomer.**

Daisy up Exercises:

Write the four principles for defeating your Giants:

Principle #1

Principle #2

Principle #3

Principle #4

Which one of these is most difficult for you? Why?

_____   _____

Take some time to draw or paint your Giant...or cut out pictures or words from magazines to describe it. Then plaster the word DEFEATED over the middle of it and write (your name)_____Giant Overcomer underneath it!

Journal Prompt:

Write about a giant you are facing right now...give it a name...what will you say to your giant? Copy the image of your giant. What will you do to defeat this giant...Be specific. Write it under the sign: **GO: GIANT OVERCOMER**

Prayer:

Lord, grant me the courage of David when he faced the giant Goliath. Give me faith to face any giant that separates me from you. No matter what happens in my life, help me to stand firm against the enemy's schemes. Help me to be a GO—Giant Overcomer in the things that bombard my soul. You are my

King, let me fight for your honor and glory. I will be courageous and I will not fear for you are on my side and will give me victory. I pray this in Jesus' name. Amen.

Quote:

"I learned that courage was not the absence of fear, but the triumph over it. The brave man is not he who does not feel afraid, but he who conquers that fear." Nelson Mandela

Day 15

DAISY UP...EMBRACING A CUP OF KINDNESS

"Be kind and compassionate to one another."

Eph.4:32

I remember multiple acts of kindness rendered during my husband's battle with ALS. People scheduled times to visit and pray with Kenny; cook meals for him; and make him laugh. A cup of kindness speaks louder than words and leaves a lasting impression. Can you remember a time when you were the recipient of someone's kindness? Doesn't it fill you with gratitude?

When we are guests in someone's home, we are often offered a cup of tea or coffee. Perhaps we can offer a cup of kindness to visitors in our homes. Kindness is one of the least talked about fruits of the Spirit yet it is the most impactful. More than anything else in our day, our world needs kindness. It is the virtue that can really make a difference in our world, because it flows out of love. The people who make a difference in your life are not the ones with the most credentials, the most wealth, or the most awards. They are the ones who show that they care.

WHAT IS KINDNESS?

Let's say it is an invitation.

> *"Be kind and compassionate to one another, forgiving each other, just as in Christ God forgave you." Eph.4:32*

Kindness means to be good, useful and helpful. It means to be considerate and gracious in all situations regardless of the circumstances. Kindness means sympathy, generosity, and benevolence. Kindness means that we find ways to brighten and cheer the lives of others. The Hebrew word -*chesed*- means to treat courteously and appropriately. It can also be translated as *"loving kindness."* The Greek word -*chestotes*- means useful, pleasant, and gracious. Kindness is caring enough about others that we treat them with gentleness, graciousness, and generosity. Kindness is an attitude that manifests itself in action and kind deeds.

Have you ever been in a situation where you regretted the words you spoke? Have you overlooked a kind deed or turned down an opportunity to help when you could have? Have you been impatient toward someone treating them with disrespect? In the aftermath, these kinds of actions can leave us sad and humbled.

WHY SHOW KINDNESS?

First, God is our source of kindness.

Second, He tells us to be kind to others.

In each of the scriptures below, circle the word **kindness.**

"Consider therefore, the kindness and sternness of God: sternness to those who fell, but kindness to you, provided that you continue in his kindness." Ro.11:22

"…in order that in the coming ages he might show the incomparable riches of his grace, expressed in his kindness to us in Christ Jesus." Eph.2:7

"…and to godliness, brotherly kindness; and to brotherly kindness, love." 2Pe.1:7

"But when the kindness and love of God our Savior appeared,
He saved us, not because of righteous things we had done,
but because of his mercy." Titus 3:4

"…in purity, understanding, patience and kindness;" 2Co.6:6
"Love is patient; love is kind." 1 Co.13:4

Third, Jesus demonstrated kindness by the way he lived. He preached the gospel to the poor, healed the sick, fed the hungry, held children on his lap, listened to their stories, raised the dead, and gave sinners a second chance.

Fourth, we should show kindness because we can.

"I can do all things through Christ who strengthens me."
Phil.4:13

TO WHOM DO WE SHOW KINDNESS?

Who's on your list? Circle any below that apply to you personally.

- Family
- Friends
- Neighbors
- Co-workers

- Church members
- Classmates, teachers, cafeteria workers
- Postmen and paper carriers
- The unlovable
- Those who don't deserve it
- The lonely
- The elderly
- The stranger on the street
- Waitresses
- Check out people at the grocery store
- Our enemies

The last one is perhaps the hardest, but it reaps the greatest reward.

"If your enemy is hungry, feed him; if he is thirsty, give him something to drink. In doing this, you will heap burning coals on his head. Do not become overcome by evil, but overcome evil with good." Ro.12:20-21

Don't be duped into taking the bait of Satan. Your small acts of kindness will eventually bear fruit. Give it a try. We are to treat others with genuine kindness because of the kindness that God has shown us in Jesus Christ. It's our turn to pay if forward.

HOW DO WE SHOW KINDNESS?

Eric Hoffer says, "We are made kind by being kind." Practice makes perfect. James, the brother of Jesus, tells us to not just talk about kindness but to put good deeds into practice.

Check the acts of kindness you already offer and write any others that apply:

- Visiting the sick, the elderly, and lonely.
- Doing favors.
- Calling the discouraged.
- Cooking meals or cleaning for someone sick or in need.
- Giving to the needy.
- Resisting the urge to gossip.
- Shoveling snow for the elderly.
- Sending a card of cheer.
- Granting forgiveness.
- Sending or picking flowers for someone.
- Passing on a great book.
- Doing kind deeds as a family.
- Serving in a soup kitchen.
- Collecting hats and gloves for poor.
- Giving a backpack of school supplies to the children in poor schools.
- Supporting our troops overseas.

- Lending a listening ear to someone in distress.
- Volunteering in hospice.
- Comforting the grieving.
- Other:_____

If you don't think the world is hungry for kindness, consider this. In 1982, activist Anne Herbert coined a phrase: *Random Acts of Kindness*. The idea took root and became very popular. In 1992, a book with that title was published asking us to imagine what would happen if there were an outbreak of kindness in the world, if everyone just started doing kind deeds every day. This idea took off in businesses, schools, churches, and homes. Why was it so successful? Because…

Kindness leaves a lasting impression.

Kindness is remembered.

Kindness goes the second mile.

Kindness goes out of its way to tell someone you care.

Kindness is a commitment.

Kindness costs something.

Kindness makes a difference.

William Penn said, "*I expect to pass through life but once. If therefore, there be any kindness I can show, or any good thing*

I can do to any fellow-human being, let it be now, and not defer or neglect it, as I shall not pass this way again."

"This is my command: Love each other." John 15:17

In *Matt.25:31-46*, we learn that at the end of time, the Lord will separate people one from the other. The sheep on his right and the goats on his left. To those on the right he will say, "Come, you who are blessed by my Father; take your inheritance, the kingdom prepared for you since the creation of the world. For I was hungry and you gave me to eat; I was thirsty and you gave me to drink; I was a stranger and you invited me in; I needed clothes and you clothed me, sick and you looked after me; in prison and you came to visit me."

They will ask him when they did these things. He tells them whenever they did it for the least of their brothers, they did it for him. Wouldn't you like to be on the sheep side? God clearly tells us that KINDNESS is the way to come into his kingdom.

Daisy up Exercises:

Today is an excellent time to make a resolution to be kind. It's so simple, isn't it? You don't need special skills, degrees, fame or fortune to be kind. Would you be willing to sign a Kindness Covenant? Make a promise to do an act of kindness for 21 days.

That's how long it takes to form a habit. Afterward, you will want to keep it going.

Pray about it and sign below:

LORD, I promise to be faithful to this Kindness Covenant. For 21 days, I will perform an act of kindness every day, for your honor and glory. Amen.

Signature: _____

Have fun filling in the acrostic below…each line can be one word or a phrase.

Kindness acrostic:
K

I

N

D

N

E

S

S

Journal Prompt:

Write about a time you were the recipient of someone's kindness. Describe it in detail and write your feelings about it. How can you pass it on to someone else?

Try writing a poem about Kindness.

Prayer:

Lord of all kindness and mercy, help me to live my life pouring out your love and kindness on others. Show me the people, times, and places where I can be of service to those less fortunate. Lord, I want to pay it forward because of the love and kindness you have shown to me in my life. It only takes a spark to get the flame going. Amen.

Quote:

"Constant kindness can accomplish much. As the sun makes ice melt, kindness causes misunderstanding, mistrust, and hostility to evaporate." Albert Schweitzer

Day 16

DAISY UP…EMBRACING THE HEART

"Will you not revive us again?"

Ps.85:6

I fondly remember my Profession Day in the convent. This was the day I made my vows of poverty, chastity, and obedience to the Lord. I received the black veil, a myrtle crown, and a ring. It was my wedding day …I was now a Bride of Christ. There are no words to describe the joy and euphoria of that day. I was passionately in love with Jesus and wanted to give my heart to him without reserve. It was one of the most extraordinary days of my life.

The choir sang these verses of *Psalm45*:

"…therefore, God, your God, has set you above your companions by anointing you with the oil of joy." v.7

"Listen, O daughter, consider and give ear; Forget your people and your father's house. The king if enthralled by your beauty, honor him, for he is your Lord." v.10-11
"They are led in with joy and gladness; they enter the palace of the king." v.16

I didn't need to revive my heart that day because it was already aflame with the love of Christ! I belonged to him! Years have gone by since that day in August of 1963. Where is my heart now? Do I need it revived? The question brought me to Genesis when God was walking through the garden after Adam and Eve sinned. He called out, *"Where are you?" Gen.3:8.* Let's imagine that God is standing before me and you at this moment and He is asking us that same question. Where are you? Are we near, halfway, or far from Him?

Let's examine each position so you and I can answer this question truthfully.

#1 NEAR

"The Lord would speak to Moses face to face as a man speaks with his friend." Ex.33:11

What comprises that kind of encounter?

- Being faithful to a daily time of prayer.
- Reading and meditating on God's Word daily.
- Keeping a spiritual journal.
- Listening to audio or podcast sermons.
- .Attending prayer meetings.
- Writing my prayers to God.
- Praying without ceasing.
- Worshiping and praising.
- Thanking him continually.

You see, Moses would speak to God, as a friend, telling him all about the people, his problems, their problems, and how he was leading them. He would listen to what God had to say to him and he would come out of this encounter with a radiant face. Just being in His Presence was all Moses wanted. I love these words of John Piper, *"God is most glorified in us when we are most satisfied in Him."*

166

#2 HALFWAY

"…and his heart was not fully devoted to the Lord as the heart of David his father had been." 1 Kings 11:4

This verse referred to Solomon in his old age as he allowed his wives to turn his heart to other gods. He wasn't completely alienated from God but he had compromised his devotion. Let's say he was halfway toward God and halfway toward idols. This is a scary position since we can become complacent and justify our behavior. This is a lukewarm position and this is not pleasing to God. *Rev.3:15-16, "I know your deeds, that you are neither cold nor hot. I wish you were either one or the other! So, because you are lukewarm-neither hot nor cold- I am about to spit you out of my mouth."*

What does lukewarm look like?

- A spiritual slump.
- Little or no quiet time with the Lord.
- Losing your love for Jesus.
- Going through the motions at church.
- Dried up and not serving.
- Quitting Bible study.
- Becoming lazy with your spiritual growth.

- Having no enthusiasm.
- Everything becomes a duty or obligation.
- Busyness and lots of distractions.

It's interesting that Solomon, the wisest man in the world, let his pagan wives lead him astray from the Lord. Who are your "pagan wives?" Who or what is leading you away from the Lord into this pool of lukewarm nothingness? Anne Graham Lotz shared about her desert and wilderness time. She said she didn't drift away from God intentionally or willingly. She just got overly busy and distracted doing things for God but not being with God. She said she lost her focus on Jesus. Then slowly, she began her journey back to God. She did it by praying the Word of God and beginning revival conferences. She said that revival is not fire and brimstone preaching but an awakening of one's relationship with God through the practice of prayer and meditation on the Word of God. If we're not on fire in our hearts for Jesus then something is seriously wrong. Listen to Anne's CD…*Just Give Me Jesus*. That will truly revive your heart.

#3 FAR

"Yet I hold this against you: You have forsaken your first love." Rev.2:4

In the first three chapters of Revelation, Jesus is speaking to the seven churches in Asia Minor. Chapter 2 is directed toward the church of Ephesus. Jesus starts out by commending the people on their good deeds, hard work, perseverance, resisting sin, not growing weary, and not tolerating false doctrines. That sounds quite praiseworthy, doesn't it? But verse four cancels out everything because they had lost their zeal and love for God.

What is first love? It is a passionate, exclusive love for Jesus. I remember the charismatic movement in the 70's and 80's. I myself still loved the Lord deeply but I had also gotten very busy doing the work of the Lord especially teaching children and being involved in parish work. But the Life in the Spirit renewal brought me back to my first love. It made me realize I was lacking fervent intimacy with God and His Word. This movement brought me to my knees and revived my heart in a remarkable way. I was especially on fire for the Word of God. I devoured it with a whole new enthusiasm and fervor. It led me back to God with passion and fire. What about you? Has someone or something brought you back to that place of First Love? Jot it your memory in the box below:

So where are you? Where is your heart? Circle the one that represents you:

NEAR   **HALFWAY**   **FAR**

If you circled halfway or far, are you wondering, how to get to NEAR?

" Remember the height from which you have fallen!
Repent and do the things you did at first. If you do not
repent, I will come to you and remove your lampstand
from its place." Rev.2:5

REMEMBER

Recall in your mind when you first came to know Jesus as Lord. Do you remember the joy, excitement, and exhilaration? You couldn't seem to get enough…hanging out with Jesus friends, studying the Bible, serving in the church, witnessing in the streets and to your family and friends. Jesus won you over heart, soul, and spirit.

REPENT

If you've lost that first love, it's not the end. Jesus gives us another chance. He tells us to repent. In other words—turn around and come back to him. If sin has entered your life, you need to confess it to the Lord and ask for forgiveness, and then leave it behind. Ask him to wash you clean and purify your heart. He wants you back in the circle of His love. There is no sin or shame too great for his saving love on the cross.

REPEAT

Do the things you did at first. Pray, worship, read and meditate on his Word, get back into right fellowship, and serve others in the body of Christ.

WARNING

If you don't return to your first love, he will remove his lampstand. In other words, he will remove his light from your life and you will no longer be effective.

Ask Jesus today to revive your heart. Pray for a deeper, more intimate relationship with him. The Word of God says that if we ask, we will receive.

I remember my dad sharing his testimony with me after attending a Cursillo..a weekend retreat in the Catholic faith. He told me that it was the first time in his life that he came to know Jesus personally. He was in love with Jesus and wanted to serve him. Jesus revived his heart.

"I will give them a heart to know me, that I am the LORD."

Jer.24:7

What about you?

Do you want to know him personally?

Do you want a fresh start?

Do you want to fall in love with Jesus all over again?

Do you want passion and fire for Jesus in your heart?

Do you want a revived heart?

Ask and you will receive! He will never withhold his love from you. He longs for you.

Daisy up Exercises:

In the verse below circle the words *"know Christ."*

"I want to know Christ and the power of his resurrection and the fellowship of sharing in his sufferings." Phil.3:10

What are 3 things you can personally do to "***Know Christ?***"

#1

#2

#3

Look over some of these suggestions to revive your heart for Jesus. Circle 3 that you could try to do over the next year.

Attend a women's retreat	Join a women's bible study	Buy a new devotional
Purchase a set of audio tapes	Attend a prayer meeting	Read a new book
Sign up for on line devotionals	Go to a conference	Get a spiritual mentor
Teach a class	Volunteer in a shelter	Write your prayers
Start a gratitude journal	Take nature walks	Take a solitude day
Join a praise team	Dance for the Lord	Write poetry

Jot down some of your own ideas:

Journal Prompt:

In your journal write the verse below:

"I will give you an undivided heart and put a new spirit in them; I will remove from them their heart of stone and give them a heart of flesh." Ezek.11:19

Draw two hearts below: One that is divided and one that is undivided…Label the divided heart –Heart of Stone. Label the undivided heart—Heart of Love.

Under the heart of stone write what is keeping you from giving Jesus your wholehearted love and devotion. Under the undivided heart write your love letter to Jesus.

Prayer:

Lord, revive my heart today. Give me a new hunger and thirst for your Word. Let me sing your praises day and night. Let me be excited to tell others about you and the joy you give to those who love you. Let me give my first time of the day solely to you. You, Lord, are my all in all. Let nothing separate me from your love. I give you my wholehearted devotion today and forever. Amen.

Quote:

"True revival is that divine moment when God bursts upon the scene and displays his glory." Del Fehsenfeld Jr.

Day 17

DAISY UP…EMBRACING VICTORY OVER TEMPTATION

"But when you are tempted, he will also provide a way out
so that you can stand up under it."
1Co.10:13

Years ago, I was a second and third grade teacher in an inner city school. There was a particular boy in my class who couldn't sit still and listen. One day while teaching a lesson, I noticed he was fussing noisily in his desk. I called out, "Daryl, what are you doing?" He looked up at me and said, "Teacher, there's a bug in my desk." I answered back, "Well, then, get that bug out of your desk and pay attention." It seemed like an ordinary situation most teachers deal with every day. But that story came to mind as I was preparing this reflection. I realized even a bug can teach us lessons. Daryl was distracted by that bug and therefore he missed most of the teaching and got into trouble because of it. The day didn't start out well for Daryl but it ended well after he got the bug out of his desk. Victory!

I think of the bug as a temptation and the desk as the mind. Do you have a bug (a temptation) in your mind that is distracting you? That temptation is the wish to do or have something which you should not do or have. Who puts the temptation in your mind? You already know the answer—The Devil. He'll bug you to death, if you let him. Because of the temptations, we can get easily distracted from our walk with Christ. The enemy makes the temptation look good and it calls our name endearingly. We check it out and lose sight of God. We start missing out on what God wants to teach us because we are yielding to temptation. We miss out on the opportunities for blessing that God is extending to us. When we start playing or toying with temptation, we will get burned. The critical thing to remember is that we can learn how to stand against temptation and find a way out. What does God have to say about man's oldest problem –temptation?

The Bible talks about two different kinds of testing. One is about trials and the other is about temptation.

- Trials are situations designed by God to help us to grow- to strengthen our character.

- Temptations are designed by the devil to cause us to sin and turn away from God.

"Blessed is the man who perseveres under trial, because when he has stood the test, he will receive the crown of life that God has promised to those who love him." James 1:12

There is a prize, a reward for persevering under trial. James calls that man blessed which means happy. Happiness comes from having your life under control, so that no bad habit is defeating you. When you learn to say "NO" to temptation it produces happiness in your life. The verse also says he will receive the crown of life. In the Greek this literally means *Life Itself*. When you understand temptation, when you overcome it, when you learn to say no, then you begin to live the abundant life God has promised to you. The burning question everyone asks is HOW? How do I handle temptation and learn to say no when I really want to say yes?

Let's look at five principles to gain victory over temptation.

#1 BE REALISTIC

James 1:13 refers to when we are tempted, not if we are tempted. Every day we're tempted. You're tempted and I'm tempted. You never get too old for it and you never get too spiritual for it. It's a reality of life and we all know the spirit is willing but the flesh is weak. And the closer we get to God the more we will be tempted.

"No temptation has seized you except what is common to man. And God is faithful; he will not let you be tempted beyond what you can bear. But when you are tempted, he will also provide a way out so that you can stand up under it." 1Co.10:13

We need to understand that it's not a sin to be tempted. It's only a sin when we give in to the temptation. Even Jesus was tempted in the desert.

"For we do not have a high priest who is unable to sympathize with our weaknesses, but we have one who has been tempted in every way, just as we are, yet was without sin." Heb.4:15

Temptation proves you're human, not evil. Remember, the Devil's goal is to turn us away from God. He wants to steal, kill, and destroy everything in your life. But God is greater than the enemy and he assures us of victory.

#2 BE RESPONSIBLE

Accept responsibility.

Don't fall in the blame game.

Don't blame other people for your problems.

Don't blame society.

Don't blame your environment.

Don't blame your heredity.

Don't blame your spouse.

Don't blame your children.

Don't blame your peers.

Don't blame God.

"No one should say, God is tempting me, for God cannot be tempted by evil, nor does he tempt anyone." James 1:13

Don't always blame the devil either saying, "The devil made me do it." Much of the time we bring it on ourselves. So avoid playing the victim card. If I'm ever going to break the bad habits that harass me, I need to be realistic and start taking responsibility for my own choices.

#3 BE READY……BE PREPARED

When temptation comes, be ready!

Peter says, *"Resist him, standing firm in the faith"* 2Pe.5:9
Jesus says, *"Pray that you will not fall into temptation"* Luke 22:40
Paul says, *"Put on the full armor of God."* Eph.6:11
My mother said, *"Trust in God, sailor, but row for the shore."*

We need to be ready and prepared. Temptation does not warn you in advance. Rather, it surprises you and catches you off guard. You are most vulnerable in your down and troubled times as well as your up and happy times. So how do we prepare for temptation? How do we get ready? We need to know the tactics of our enemy. The devil is consistent and uses the same bag of tricks. So we have to catch him at his own game. We need to know the devil's schemes and use the authority Christ has given us to demolish strongholds. It doesn't happen just one time. It's something we need to repeat over and over again. Unfortunately, the enemy will never stop trying to tempt us, but we can gain the victory consistently in Christ.

The book of James outlines four steps the devil uses to tempt you.

FIRST STEP OF TEMPTATION IS: DESIRE

"Each one is tempted when, by his own evil desire."
James 1:14

It's an inside job! Many of our wants and desires are just fine. God places those desires in our heart. We couldn't live without them. But any desire that grows out of control becomes destructive. Satan likes to take routine, legitimate desires and turn them in runaway desires. You become consumed and obsessed with them. When they are out of control you know it. I find myself saying, "Houston, we have a problem!" It's often the fulfillment of a legitimate desire in the wrong way, at the wrong time. It starts with desire. For example, as Christians we know that sex outside of marriage is wrong. Our permissive society and peers say it's okay because everybody does it, but the Word of God says it's wrong. My novice mistress used to say, "What's wrong is wrong if everybody does it; what's right is right if nobody does it." Who are you going to believe? If you've failed in this area, take heart, you can be redeemed, loosened from shame, and made clean again.

SECOND STEP OF TEMPTATION IS: DECEPTION

"…but each one is tempted when, by his own evil desire, he is dragged away and enticed." James 1:14

The word "dragged away" is a hunter's term which literally means "snared into a trap." The word "enticed" is a fisherman's term which means "lured by bait." What kind of bait does the devil use on you? How does he entice you to sin? You need to know the answer to that question. He knows your triggers and vulnerabilities and he knows where and when to strike. Too often we see the hook and we know it's a temptation but we keep right on nibbling with temptation. You can't negotiate with the devil. You can't say, "Oh, I'm an adult. I know how far I can go." If you think you can keep on walking down "Bug Street" hanging out with other bugs, you are deceived. Playing with bugs is a lose —lose situation.

THIRD STEP OF TEMPTATION IS: DISOBEDIENCE

"Then, after desire has conceived, it gives birth to sin."
James 1:15

What begins in your mind results in an action. It starts in your imagination. The battle always starts with your thoughts.

First the devil gets your attention, then he gets you to have an attitude, then he gets you to commit the action. Once you cross over the line…you are ZAPPED IN THE TRAP! What starts in your mind comes out in your life and what you flirt with, you will fall for.

FOURTH STEP OF TEMPTATION IS: DEATH

"…and sin, when it is full-grown, gives birth to death."
James 1:15

Losing the battle causes devastating results. The wages of sin are death which is spiritual separation from God. There will always be consequences to my actions and decisions. I may choose to have my kicks, but there will be kickbacks.

Every time I choose to give in to temptation and sin, it will not just affect me but also those I love. Then we wish we could go back and undo our mistakes.

#4 BE REFOCUSED

If temptation begins with our inner thoughts then changing what we think about is the key to overcoming it. The primary way to overcome temptation is not to fight it. You simply need to refocus your thoughts. Change your attention. Look elsewhere. It's been said that when crows attack hawks, the hawks don't counter-attack they simply soar higher. Put on the mind of Christ. Because the more you fight a feeling the more it grabs you. Ice cream, chocolate, alcohol, drugs etc. Don't focus on what you don't want. Focus on what you want!

If you are sick, speak words of healing.
If you are worried, speak words of trust.
If you are poor, speak words of supply and abundance.
If you are self-doubting, speak words of faith.
If you are troubled, speak words of peace.
If you are sad, speak words of praise.

Put God's Word in your mind and refocus! It is our greatest weapon. Quit fighting the feeling. What you resist, persists. But if you ignore it, it will surely weaken.

My friend, Margaret Slabach wrote a beautiful haiku poem about fighting temptation.

Dangerous Warrior
Equipped with God's Living Word
Inflicting damage.

Don't try to argue with the devil. When temptation calls, drop the receiver. Don't negotiate or compromise. Physically remove yourself from the situation. When Joseph was caught in a compromising situation, he left his cloak and ran. He got out of there like the speed of lightning. You may have to change your job. You may have to change the television channel. You may have to leave some relationships. You may have to get the "bugs" out of your house. Just do whatever it takes.

#5 BE REBORN

The single most important principle in breaking bad habits and getting control of your life is to let God have control of it. Receive him in your life so you can start changing your character. Then you will have a new capacity to resist temptation.

You cannot do this on your own. You need Jesus in your life.
You need his supernatural power.
That's what it means to be reborn.
You need to be filled with the Holy Spirit.
It means you get a fresh start on life.

That can start today…this very moment. If you are struggling with temptation, tell someone you can trust. Ask for their prayers and for their help to keep you accountable. Most important…ask God to help you gain victory over temptation. Believe that he will answer your prayer and you will be restored. I read somewhere that Judas followed Christ, but that he never fully gave his heart to Christ! Let's not make the same mistake.

Daisy up Exercises:

Look at the list of temptations below: Which ones apply to you?

- Envy or jealousy
- Gossip
- Anger
- Over spending
- Alcohol
- Drugs
- Immoral behavior
- Pornography
- Lying
- Cheating
- Eating disorder
- Chocolates, sweets, snacks
- Gambling

Now take a large sheet of newsprint: With a marker divide it into 4 parts.

In the 1st box write your most vulnerable area of temptation…your weak spot. You can even draw or paste a picture of it from a magazine. In the 2nd box write what you do when your temptation comes? What are your usual responses?

In the 3rd box make a list of 3-5 things you can do to overcome the temptation.

In the 4th box…write a scripture from today's lesson that can strengthen you and help you resist the temptation.

Journal Prompt:

Name or list a few of your temptations. After each one, write what your life would look like if you gained victory over that temptation. This will be a motivational exercise.

Prayer:

Lord, you know the areas where I've stumbled. I admit it. I name it before you right now_____. I want a clean slate. I want to start over. I want to get free of the past. I ask for your forgiveness and mercy. My desire is to obey you in all things, no matter what the cost. I repent of my sins and recommit my heart to you this day and ask you to be Lord over every area of my life. I want to be wholly devoted to you- I give you my HEART!

Quote:

"Temptation is the devil looking through the keyhole. Yielding is opening the door and inviting him in." Billy Sunday

DAY 18

DAISY UP...EMBRACING THE TOUCH OF JESUS

"If I just touch his clothes, I will be healed."

Mark 5:28

*T*here are so many things in our society today that call out for a touch love or kindness. We are surrounded on all sides by hardship, hatred, bigotry, violence and oppression. Our world needs a touch of love, kindness, and acceptance. Consider these expressions of touch...

touch-squeeze toys

staples easy touch

soft touch

gentle touch

one touch

touch life

keep in touch

moms in touch

a touch of class

touch up

touch n go	midas touch
miracle touch	special touch
healing touch	touch football
finishing touch	final touch
magic touch	don't touch
touched by an angel	please touch
touch life	personal touch

The truth is that people need to be touched. We're told that babies left untouched will begin to wither away physically and emotionally. Today our story is about a woman who reached out and touched JESUS and her life was never the same again. It's found in Mark 5:25-34

"...and a large crowd followed and pressed around him and a woman was there who had been subject to bleeding for 12 years. She had suffered a great deal under the care of many doctors and had spent all she had, yet instead of getting better she grew worse." Mark 5:24-26

Let's consider three things about this woman's story:
Condition
Cure
Confession

#1 CONDITION

- She was a woman with no name—insignificant.
- She had an issue of blood for 12 years.
- She endured a lot of suffering and pain.
- She felt life draining out of her.
- She found no doctors that could heal her.
- She spent all her money on treatments.
- She was only getting worse.
- She was considered unclean.
- She wasn't allowed to touch anyone—deprived
- She could not be a wife; could not be near her children; no hugs; no kisses.
- She could not cook or clean.
- She could not go to the synagogue or ceremonies.
- She could not mingle in public.
- She was labeled "Unclean; untouchable."
- She was isolated and ostracized.
- She was as good as dead.

#2 CURE   *Mark 5:27-32*

- She had heard about Jesus and she was desperate.
- Hope was awakened.

- Faith was aroused.
- She was convinced that Jesus could help her.

"If I just touch his clothes, I will be healed." v.28.

She took the risk and stepped out. She didn't care who was watching, as she angled her way through the crowd until she could touch his garment. Such bravery deserves a resounding, "Bravo!" Ray van Lender says it was a common belief that when the Messiah came he would have healing powers in the tassels of his robe. He points out that this woman's act was an act of faith because she believed that Jesus was the Messiah. The moment she touched his garment she felt the issue of blood stop and she knew she was healed. This woman, by her act of faith, drew power from Jesus even in the midst of the crowd.

There are 2 types of healing:

- Immediate…healing happens immediately.
- Progressive…healing happens over a period of time.

"At once Jesus realized that power had gone out from him. He turned around in the crowd and asked, 'Who touched my clothes?'" v.30

Who touched my clothes? The Greek word for touched means to touch and hold on. Jesus knew somebody made a connection. Somebody got what they came for. The woman did not doubt, but believed. You can also touch his garment and hold on till you get what you ask for.

#3 CONFESSION

"Then the woman, knowing what had happened to her, came and fell at his feet and trembling with fear, told him the whole truth." Mark 5:33

- She gave her testimony.
- She spoke the honest truth.
- She was bold and courageous.
- She didn't look at the consequences.

Whatever our issue of blood is, we need to name it and acknowledge it in order to be healed. Imagine Jesus asking, *"What do you want me to do for you?"*

#4 JESUS RESPONSE

He did not...

- Rebuke her for interrupting him.
- Rebuke her for breaking Levitical law.
- Move away from her.
- Tell her to make an appointment.
- Make her feel unworthy.

Instead, He rewarded her and praised her for her faith.

"Daughter, your faith has healed you. Go in peace and be freed from your suffering." Mark 5:34

- This was the only time recorded in the scriptures that Jesus used the term daughter.
- The relationship had changed between them.
- She had gone from a nobody to a somebody.
- This was a physical healing but also a soul healing as well.
- He sent her forth in peace.

The idea expressed by the verb tense used here means to be continually healed. If Jesus has healed you of anything, don't let the enemy steal it. Keep on proclaiming it no matter what is manifesting in your body and soul. He never takes back his healing.

Perhaps some of you can identify with the woman in this story.

Do you need a touch from Jesus today? ___yes ___no

What is your issue of blood?

What separates you from others and from God?

What is draining the life out of you? Circle any that apply to you.

- Feeling insignificant and unworthy.
- A chronic illness.
- Mental illness.
- A sin that you can't give up.
- Emotional trauma.
- Depression.
- Unbelief.
- Living in abusive relationships.
- Addictions.
- Weight problems.
- A physical deformity.
- other?_____

Come as you are! Take courage like this woman. Stir up hope…believe…and reach out to touch Jesus. Whatever it is Jesus is here for you today. He is Jehovah Rapha, your healer.

EXPECT   BELIEVE   RECEIVE

"Everything is possible for him who believes." Mark 9:23

Jesus loved to touch people. In scriptures there are accounts of 27 individual healings and 10 occasions of healings of larger numbers. Jesus is still healing today through you and me.

"He called his twelve disciples to him and gave them authority to drive up evil spirits and to heal every disease and sickness." Matt.10:1

"…they will lay hands on sick people and they will get well." Mark 16:18

"Is anyone of you sick? Call the elders of the church to pray over him and anoint him with oil in the name of the Lord." James 5:14

Jesus asks us to believe. He is in charge…He is sovereign. We do not need to worry about the results. We just need to pray and to believe. Let's be brave and dare to step out like the woman with the issue of blood. That's when miracles happen. I want one, don't you?

Daisy up Exercises:

If you are sick, ask Jesus to heal you.

If you are sick, ask someone to pray for you.

If you know of someone who is sick, ask if you can pray for them.

Send a get well card or visit someone in the hospital or nursing home.

Cook a meal, clean house, do laundry, or bring flowers for someone who is sick, elderly, or aging.

Journal Prompt:

Lord, today, I come before you with my issue of blood _____.

Name it…describe how it makes you feel…how you struggle with it. Write a prayer asking Jesus to heal you as you touch the hem of his garment.

Prayer:

Lord, I thank you that you are my healer. Today, I want to be brave and come forward to touch the hem of your garment, believing and trusting that you will heal me. I've struggled so long with this condition, Lord. Your word says that you hear and answer our prayers. Your healing power is as present today as it was back when you walked this earth. I choose today to be healed in your name. Amen

Quote:

"The wound is the place where the Light enters you." *Rumi*

DAY 19

DAISY UP...EMBRACING YOUR ISAAC

"Sometime later, God tested Abraham."

Gen.22:1

*H*ave you ever read a story that made a powerful impact on your life? Intuitively you knew that God brought it to you awareness at the right time in your life. That's how I felt when I read *Lay My Isaac Down* by Carol Kent. The story begins with Utopia and ends with tragedy changed into hope. That's quite a formula isn't it? Carol reminisces about an evening walk with her husband Gene along the shores of Lake Michigan. She remembers saying to her husband, "Does life get any better than this?" Her husband's business was flourishing, her writing and speaking ministry was full of promise, and their son Jason Paul was graduating from the naval academy and being assigned to Hawaii. Life was good—almost magical.

Then the unthinkable happened with a call at the midnight hour. It was from a jail in Florida telling them that their son was arrested for first degree murder. At that moment in time, Gene and Carol's lives were changed forever. There was no turning back. Carol says this was her Isaac…their only son whom they loved…and they had to lay him on the altar.

Can you find yourself in this story? All of us, at some point in time, have had circumstances or situations that have caused us personal loss and devastation. What do you do when your life literally falls apart and you find yourself crying out to God saying, "I can't handle this?" Of course, we have a choice how to respond:

Will we choose unshakeable faith?

Will we give up on God?

Will we question God?

Will we doubt God?

Will we blame God?

Will we get angry with God?

Will we wander away from God?

There's a familiar story in Scripture that demonstrates the hidden power of God in unthinkable circumstances. It's told in Gen.22:1-19. Let's look at this story in 4 parts.

Part I TESTING v.1 & 2

"Sometime later God tested Abraham. Take your son, your only son, Isaac, whom you love and go to the region of Moriah. Sacrifice him there as a burnt offering on one of the mountains I will tell you about."

God tests us in order to confirm our faith or prove our commitment

How about you? Have you ever had a time when God tested you and it became a defining moment or a turning point in your life?

What is an Isaac? An Isaac is a gift from God; a cherished person, a treasured possession, a life-long dream, a talent, a career or gift that you need to surrender to God so that He can release his power in your life.

"The Lord gave and the Lord has taken away. May the name of the Lord be praised." Job 1:21

There are two kinds of Isaacs:

Some Isaacs are hurled upon us leaving us without any power or control.

- Terminal illness.
- Death of a loved one.
- Loss of a job.
- Financial ruin…bankruptcy.
- A burning house.
- An unwanted move.
- Divorce.
- Imprisonment.
- Result of natural disasters: tornados, earthquakes, fire, floods.

Some Isaacs are our personal choice.

- Giving up a cherished dream for a greater good.
- Doing what it takes to be set free from addictions.
- Letting your children go.
- Forgiving a person who has hurt you deeply.
- Giving up an unhealthy desire for money and material possessions.
- Giving up a sin or bad habit.

ISAACS are the heart sacrifices that we make when we choose to surrender control and honor God with our choices even when our world is shattered and shaken.

We have to decide if we will let go of our control over a particular person or situation and say yes to God or if we will hang on for dear life and refuse to relinquish something or someone we cherish saying no to God.

Part 2 What was Abraham's Response? v.3-10

#1   Immediate/ prompt obedience

Scripture says he set out the next morning. He didn't negotiate with God. There was no room to negotiate, "Deal or no deal." He just obeyed. How many times do we try to bargain with God? How many times do we get angry or bitter about something God asks of us? How many times do we become rebellious and refuse to obey because the sacrifice is too great? We've all been there haven't we?

#2   Belief/ Faith in God

Now Abraham knew that God hated human sacrifice. He knew that if God asked him to kill his son, then he would resurrect him. *"Against all hope, Abraham in hope believed and so became the father of many nations." Ro.4:18.* Abraham believed in the promise and character of God. He believed all this because of His intimate relationship with God. Unbelief talks to itself while belief talks to God.

Part 3 God's Response v.11-17

- God spared his son.

  "Now I know that you fear God because you have not withheld from me your only son." Gen.22:12

- God provided a sacrifice.

  "Abraham looked up and there in a thicket he saw a ram caught by its horns." Gen.22: 13

- God gave a blessing.

  God renewed his promise to Abraham to bless him and make his descendants as numerous as the stars. When we have a willing heart, let go and give it over to God, He will give back to us in the form of a blessing.

God laid down His Isaac, his son Jesus, whom He loved, to save us from our sins and to offer us eternal life. Sometimes when we look around us there are tragedies that are too big for a heart to hold…

9-1-1 the Bombing of the Twin Towers.

The killing at Columbine.

Persecutions in Rawanda, Darfur, and Sudan.

Amish girls killed in a schoolhouse.

Hurricane Katrina.

Earthquake in Haiti .

Tsunami in Japan.

And what about our own personal losses? The death of a child, a spouse, a divorce, financial ruin, heartbreak, addictions, sin, abuse and violence. How do you cope with something like that? How do you get through it? How do you respond in unspeakable circumstances?

I remember when my blissful life reached a turning point. It was the day my husband –my soul mate-and best friend was diagnosed with Lou Gehrig's disease. We were bluntly told that he had 2 to 5 years to live. I cried tears of raw grief for a whole week and felt like I was hanging in mid-air with no net beneath me. But God gave us a life line.

Dt.30:19-20 "…Today, I set before you, life and death, blessings and curses. Now choose life, so that you and your children may live. And that you may love the Lord your God, listen to His voice and hold fast to Him…for the Lord is your life."

We chose LIFE and learned to take one day at a time and embrace it with gratitude. We learned to hold fast to God and his Word and praise Him in the midst of our agony. Don't be like the rich young man in Matt.19 who couldn't give up his riches and went away sad.

Let's return to our opening story about Jason Paul. What happened to him? Even though Florida has the death penalty he was spared and given life imprisonment. He became assistant to the chaplain and began Bible studies in the prison. Gene and Carol had to learn a new normal. They learned about the desperate needs of prisoners and their families and started an organization to give them HOPE.

Hopefully, God has stirred your hearts today. In even the most horrific circumstances, God is at work and can bring about a greater good. It is in our actions that we show God where our heart is in relation to Him. We can pray with Jesus. *"Father, if you are willing, take this cup from me, yet not my will, but yours be done." Luke 22:42*

Daisy up Exercises:

What is your Isaac? Identify something or someone you cherish. Let go of control over the person, situation or event as an act of worship.
Embrace God's love in the process.

Rest in the outcome even if we don't understand why this is happening.

Continue to seek God's will in your time of prayer.

Be sure you seek support from family, friends, and church.

Write the name of your Isaac on the altar below. Lay your Isaac down on.

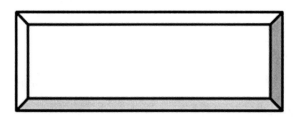

Take comfort in the fact that once we lay our Isaac down, God will resurrect and restore it to us in ways beyond our comprehension. Learn to believe and trust in his promises.

Journal Prompt and Prayer:

Finish this prayer:

Lord, today I lay my Isaac down on this altar. It is (name your Isaac) _____ .I'm feeling (list all your feelings about this situation)_____.

I'm praying for more hope and faith in this difficult time, Lord. Help me to trust your unfailing love and compassion. I won't hide this or isolate myself. I promise to find someone to confide in for prayer support and encouragement. (name that person or persons) _____. Lord, I know you work all things to our good even when we don't understand it. I surrender to your will in this matter and hold fast to your love and your strength. May you be praised in the highest! Amen.

Quote:

"God doesn't tell us what He's going to do, but He tells us who He is."
Oswald Chambers

DAY 20

DAISY UP…EMBRACING THE GOOD FIGHT

"Fight the good fight of faith."
1 Tim.6:12

Whenever I think about a fight, I remember the Rocky movie and it's amazing theme song. It stirs up my determination and strength to face the things I must fight in my life. As a little girl, growing up in the projects, I'd walk out to the end of our sidewalk, put up my little fists, and ask every passerby if they "wanna fight?" I have no idea where that came from but I did it more often than my mom liked. I also remember a boxing match between me and another girl set up by my brother. Bill had trained me for months to box and wrestle so I could defend myself against bullies. There were about 50 kids at the event to cheer us on. After sparring a bit, I punched the other girl in the nose. She threw her gloves down and went home crying. My brother proudly proclaimed me the winner and all the other kids gained a holy fear of me. When I think back about that incident, I'm proud of that little fighter girl. She had spunk and did what she had to do to survive. She wasn't going to be intimidated. She went on the offensive instead of the defensive. I'm not proud I punched someone in the face, but the other girl was a willing participant in the fight and evidently thought she could win. It still gives me incentive to fight the good fight when I want to throw take off my gloves and give up. Perhaps God was preparing me to fight the battles I'd face in spiritual warfare.

Spiritual warfare encompasses the world, the flesh, and the devil. Paul tells us in Eph.6 to put on the full armor of God. But today I want to focus on 2 weapons of spiritual warfare. The defensive weapon which is the shield of faith and the offensive weapon which is the sword of the Spirit. The most important thing to remember is this: Always be ready! Always be prepared for battle.

SHIELD OF FAITH

"Above all, take up the shield of faith, with which you can extinguish all the flaming arrows of the evil one." Eph.6:16

What does a Roman shield look like?

- It's oblong, door-shaped, wide and long.
- It completely covered the soldier's body.
- It was made of wood covered with many layers of thick leather.
- It was extremely tough and durable.
- It could become stiff and breakable over time if not properly taken care of.

Every morning, the soldiers had a ritual of soaking a piece of cloth with oil and rubbing the ointment into the leather portion of the shield to keep it soft and pliable. If a soldier neglected this task, he was asking for certain death since the leather would harden and crack and fall to pieces. The amazing thing about these shields is that they could interlock with each other allowing the soldiers to form an impenetrable wall against the enemy both in front and in back and also over their heads to obstruct the fiery darts from passing through. Before battle, the soldier would douse his shield with water to divert spears, arrows, and fiery darts. What an impressive sight.

How does this apply to our lives? We too are in a battle against our enemy the devil and and we need the shield of faith, the complete covering of God to protect us.

"The Lord is my strength and my shield." Ps.28:7

"Do not be afraid, Abram. I am your shield, your very great reward." Gen.15:1

The lesson to remember is that we also need frequent, daily anointing of the Holy Spirit. Without a fresh touch of the Spirit, our faith would become stiff and brittle. Before battle, we need to splash our faith with believing prayer and the Word of God.

Faith is an unwavering belief and trust in God. And the purpose of our shield of faith is to extinguish the fiery darts aimed at us from the enemy. These fiery darts were arrows dipped in oil and shot from a bow with the intention of setting you on fire.

What are the fiery darts of our enemy?

fear	doubt	anger	guilt
shame	pride	greed	despair and others

The enemy's goal is to attack our mind, heart, body and soul. We can respond in three ways:

- Run away.
- Stand still paralyzed with fear.
- Move ahead and advance toward the enemy.

Sometimes when we see the enemy advancing we want to turn around and run. We want to give in and quit. We doubt God's power and we focus only on the fiery dart. We lose sight of God and let down our shield. But the scriptures are very clear about what we are to do: **STAND FIRM**

"Be on your guard; stand firm in the faith; be men of courage; be strong." 1 Co.16:13
"It is by faith you stand firm." 2 Co.1:24

So don't be afraid. Hold up your shield of faith. Stand firm and believe in the Lord and his mighty power to save. Don't be afraid of the vast army coming against you. The Lord will fight the battle for you. Take up your position and stand firm.

"No weapon forged against you will prevail, and you will refute every tongue that accuses you." Isa.54:17

TAKE UP YOUR SHIELD OF FAITH

- Exercise your faith and it will grow stronger every day.
- Be faithful and consistent in prayer.
- Be filled with the Holy Spirit.
- Be in God's Word every day.
- Gather with others for praise and worship.

Those without the shield of Faith are running around in the battle unprotected and inviting sure attack and death from the enemy.

SWORD OF THE SPIRIT

"Take the sword of the spirit which is the Word of God."
Eph.6:17

In this passage, Paul is not referring to the whole Bible. The sword is the Spirit and the Spirit is the spoken Word of God which is our sword. It was the offensive weapon.

Various swords used by the Roman Army:

- Huge double-handed sword. This was a sword so massive it could only be held with both hands. It was basically used in practice since it was too awkward for real battle. The soldiers used it to strengthen their muscles.
- Long sword. This was used for fighting in battle. It was effective but would simply wound a soldier rather than kill him.
- Small dagger. In the Greek it was called *machaira*. This is the sword that Paul speaks of in *Eph.6:17*. It caused great fear in the minds of those who heard it. It was a weapon

of murder that caused excruciating pain as the victim lay bleeding to death on the battlefield. It was a brutal weapon, less than 19 inches long. It was short and shaped like a dagger. It could only be used in close combat. The tip turned upward like a corkscrew and shredded the insides. Sounds awful, doesn't it?

The Holy Spirit , the Word of God, is the Sword. "Word" used in this passage is taken from the Greek *"rhema"* which is a quickened word—an utterance of God given by the Holy Spirit in our heart. When you receive a *rhema* —the Holy Spirit drops a word or scripture into your heart causing it to come alive in a supernatural way. It imparts special power and authority within you. Keeping that in mind read *Heb.4:12 "...for the word (rhema) of God is living and active, sharper than any double-edged sword."* Double means "two-mouthed." The word of God is like a sword that has 2 edges cutting both ways and doing terrible damage to the enemy. Let's look at an example: You are praying about a serious situation when suddenly a Bible verse comes to mind. You are consciously aware that God has given you a verse to stand on and to pray over your situation. When my husband was dying of ALS, the Spirit gave us *Dt.30:19-20.* You receive a word right out of the mouth of God and it settles into your spirit. It's a word so sharp it cuts right through your intellect , reasoning, and questions. It becomes lodged deep in your heart. After you meditate on that *rhema* word, it suddenly begins to release its power inside of you. You need to say it out loud. When you do this, those mighty words are sent forth like a powerful sword to drive back the attacks of the enemy aimed against you, your family, your marriage, your finances, your relationships, or your health.

First the word came out of the mouth of God. Second, the word came out of your mouth. Then it became a sharp two-edged sword. The Word of God remains a single edged sword when it comes out of the mouth of God and drops into your heart but is never released from your own mouth by faith. That *rhema* word lies asleep in your heart never becoming the two-edged sword God designed it to be. Something happens in your spirit when you finally rise up and begin to speak forth that word. The moment it comes out of your mouth a second edge is added to the blade. Nothing is more powerful than a word that first comes from the mouth of God and then from your mouth. There is nothing more powerful than praying and saying God's word out loud. This action releases God's mighty power into the situation at hand.

"He made my mouth like a sharpened sword." Isa.49:2

"In his hand he held 7 stars and out of his mouth came a sharp double-edged sword." Rev.1:16

Use your Sword:

- Read and study the scriptures.
- Pray for divine enlightenment.
- Memorize scripture—hide it in your heart.
- Meditate on His Word.
- Speak his Word out loud.
- Share the Word with others.

When you are tempted and things seem to go from bad to worse; when discouragement rears its ugly head, when fear paralyzes you, take a deep breath and remember that you are not alone. You have God, his Word, your church, your family and friends to stand with you to fight the good fight.

Daisy up Exercises:

Write the word FAITH in the shield below.

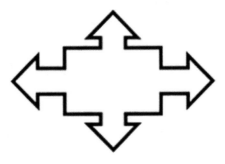

Raise your shield and pray this out loud:

There is nothing too difficult for my God. In the name of my Savior Jesus Christ, I rebuff these fiery darts and ask for the strength to advance courageously forward in faith and trust, never doubting, that God is at my side.

Raise your sword (draw one in the space below) and pray this out loud:

I confess that God's word is a sharp two-edged sword that releases its power when I speak it out of my mouth. I read the word; I take it deeply into my heart; and then I release its power from my mouth to thwart the enemy's plan and to bring victory into every situation I'm facing.

Journal Prompt:

The spiritual warfare I am now facing is…
The verse from the Bible that God has given me is…
I feel God is saying to me …..

Prayer:

Father God, empower me with your Holy Spirit. In every attack against me personally or against my loved ones, help me to raise the shield of faith and the sword of the Spirit against the enemies of darkness. May your Words put them to flight and may I stand firm proclaiming your power and might. With you there is victory for the righteous. I receive that in Jesus' name. Amen.

Quote:

"It's not the size of the dog in the fight, it's the size of the fight in the dog." Mark Twain

DAY 21

DAISY UP...EMBRACING THE PARALYTIC

"...whoever is kind to the needy honors God."

Prov.14:31

Many of us don't realize the degree of influence we exert in others' lives. It's called power and it can be used to significantly make a difference in someone's life. It's a result of living and loving like Jesus. That's what Jesus did every day in the marketplace. It's astounding that we too can make a differ-ence in someone's life by a sincere smile, a helping hand, an offered prayer, or a word of praise or encouragement.

Today, let's look at a story in the Bible that demonstrates how four friends made an incredible and life-changing difference in a man's life. They could have looked the other way or pretended not to notice the man's dilemma. How often we tend to look the other way rather than lend a helping hand. The scene opens in *Mark 1:1-2.* *"A few days later, when Jesus again entered Capernaum, the people heard that he had come home. So many gathered that there was no room left, not even outside the door, and he preached the word to them."* Some scholars believe that Jesus was actually in Peter's house that day. Among the people gathered to be near him, were Pharisees and teachers of the law from every village in Galilee, Judea and Jerusalem. You can imagine everyone hanging on to his words as he spoke to them. To get the full appreciation of this story, let's divide it into five parts.

Part 1 ACTION OF FRIENDS

*"Some men came bringing to him a paralytic, carried
by four of them. Since they could not get him to Jesus
because of the crowd, they made an opening in the roof
above Jesus, and after digging through it, lowered the mat
the paralyzed man was lying on."* Mark 2:3-4

What do we observe in these verses? What were the actions of these friends?

- A man who was paralyzed.
- Four friends who loved and cared about him.

- They heard Jesus was at this house and seized the opportunity to reach out.
- They interrupted their personal agendas to help their friend.
- They worked as a team.
- They were determined to get their friend there.
- They couldn't get through the crowd so they climbed to the roof.
- They tackled a difficult task digging an opening through the roof.
- They lowered the man right in front of Jesus.

Possibly you've known someone who was paralyzed or in a wheel chair. They are helpless in certain areas and need the hands of others. At our women's retreat we had a young woman in a wheel chair. There was no way for her to get down to the meeting room in the lower level. Four women took turns carrying her and the wheelchair down the stairs. I can assure you it was a daunting task, but it was done with unselfish love. And it made all the difference in this woman's life to be able to attend the retreat. There are times we may experience spiritual paralysis brought on by sickness, guilt, fear, trials, loneliness, trauma, isolation, sin, or even self-pity. This can be far more devastating than physical paralysis. If you've been in this state of mind, then you know the feeling of hopelessness it brings. Or perhaps you know someone who is spiritually paralyzed. What are you doing about it? Are you like one of these friends? Do you push your way through the obstacles to lend a hand. You have the power to make a huge difference in someone's life by bringing them to Jesus. Ask God whom you might help? He will answer you.

Part 2 The Answer of Jesus

" When Jesus saw their faith, he said to the paralytic,
'Son, your sins are forgiven.'" Mark 2:5

Jesus saw the faith of the four friends and of the paralytic, and he was impressed. *"Without faith it is impossible to please God." Heb.11:6. Jesus was pleased to see their* faith. But then Jesus completely surprises everyone by going to the source of the man's problem and forgiving him his sin. Why would he do that when the crowd expected him to perform a miracle and simply heal the man? Because Jesus knew his deepest need was forgiveness. Forgiveness is the power to set someone free from past sin or offense, and restore to an individual a sense of self-worth. This is something we all need at one time or another in our lives.

An unforgiving spirit is also a paralysis. The person who won't forgive is paralyzed. He can't move on in his life. He's lying on the cot just like the paralyzed man. Is there someone in your life you need to forgive today? Or is there someone you need to ask forgiveness of? Do you have the courage to say, "I'm sorry. Please forgive me?" That takes a lot of character, doesn't it? But Jesus is all about forgiveness. Just do it and experience the peace and joy that will follow.

Part 3 The Attitude of the Pharisees

"Now some teachers of the law were sitting there, thinking to themselves, 'Why does this fellow talk like that? He's blaspheming! Who can forgive sins but God alone?'" Mark 2:6-7

These were the self-righteous ones—learned and legalistic. They tithed, fasted, and prayed three times a day. They were arrogant and unbelieving. Jesus was a threat to them and they wanted to catch him in a mistake. Notice they were murmuring in their hearts. It makes us question our own hearts. Have we been filled with pride and arrogance when someone has surpassed us? Have you ever murmured in your heart against someone? Have you compared yourself to another, thinking you were much better than them? Have you ever entertained a critical, negative attitude? It's a miserable way to live, isn't it? We have to make up our minds to let go of anything that is self-righteous, critical, or judgmental. Let's allow God to be the judge. That will take a load off your shoulders. Whew!

Part 4 The Power of Forgiveness

Immediately Jesus knew in his spirit that this was what they were thinking in their hearts, and he said to them, "Why are you thinking these things? Which is easier: to say to the paralytic, 'Your sins are forgiven,' or to say, 'Get up, take your mat and walk'? But that you may know that the Son of Man has authority on earth to forgive sins." So he said to the man, "I tell you, get up, take your mat and go home." He got up, took his mat and walked out in full view of them all. This amazed everyone and they praised God, saying, "We have never seen anything like this!" Mark 2:8-11

C.S. Lewis says that the most important thing about Jesus is that He is God. But obviously, the Pharisees didn't believe that. Jesus wasn't about to debate with them. He simply manifested his authority and power to forgive sins by healing this man of his paralysis. Jesus says the same to you and me. My son, my daughter, your sins are forgiven. Take up your mat and walk. We don't have to lay on our cots feeling helpless, guilty, shamed, or rejected. He reaches out to you in unconditional love. Accept Jesus' sacrifice on the cross, receive His forgiveness, and live a full abundant life.

Part 5 The Amazement of the Crowd

"He got up, took his mat and walked out in full view of them

all. This amazed everyone and they praised God, saying,

"We have never seen anything like this." Mark 2:12

Perhaps no one would have been amazed that day if the paralytic had not obeyed the command of Jesus. He got up in faith and began to walk. He was healed at the moment he obeyed Jesus and everyone praised God.

When God asks us to do something for Him, instead of making excuses, why not step out in faith and obey. See what only God can do in your life. People are watching you and will be inspired as you live out your calling to live and love like Jesus. There are a lot of things you do that won't matter ten years from now. But touching a life, making a difference, that's worth remembering! I want to show up in the arena of life—don't you?

Daisy up Exercises:

Who will you bring to Jesus today? Pretend that this shape below is a cot:

Write the name of someone you know who is paralyzed—physically, spiritually, or emotionally. Write their name on the cot then jot down things you can do for them that will make a difference in their lives.

For example:

- Pray for them every day for a specific period of time.
- Invite them to lunch.
- Send them a 'thinking about you card'.
- Text them a word of encouragement or a scripture.
- Watch a comedy with them.
- Surprise them with an act of kindness.

Put your "cot card" at the feet of Jesus. Watch what he will do through your acts of kindness. Believe that you can make a difference in someone's life today.

Journal Prompt:

Finish this declaration of kindness with 10 things you can do to make a difference:

I Declare that I will make a difference in someone's life by acts of kindness:

#1

#2

#3

#4

#5

#6

#7

#8

#9

#10

Prayer:

Lord, show me what to do today to make a difference in someone's life. Help me to step out of my comfort zone and help others who are in need. Nudge me to make a phone call, send a card, or visit someone in person. Whatever I need to do, may it bring comfort, joy, and peace into someone's life. I want to have the heart of these four friends and interrupt the busyness of my life to show an act of kindness. Thank you for this opportunity. I pray this in Jesus' name. Amen.

Quote:

"The world is not interested in what we do for a living. What they are interested in is what we have to offer freely- hope, strength, love and the power to make a difference".
Sasha Azevedo

The world is not interested in what we do for a living. What they are interested in is what we have to offer freely- hope, strength, love and the power to make a difference.

Sasha Azevedo

DAY 22

DAISY UP…EMBRACING GETHSEMANE

"My Father, if it is possible, may this cup be taken away from me, yet not as I will, but as you will." Matt.26:39

*T*here is so much I want to say to you today and I have struggled with how to say it, so I decided to simply share from my heart. Some of you know my story. In summary, I spent thirty years of my life as a nun. Then God called me out to serve him in this world. A few years later, I married Kenny Moore, my best friend and soul mate. We eventually came to High Mill Church of the Resurrection in Canton, Ohio where I served as an ordained pastor and my husband served as a deacon. In the seventh year of our marriage, Kenny was diagnosed with ALS (Lou Gehrig's disease). In an instant our lives changed, dreams were shattered, and faith was strengthened. After three years, on Super Bowl Sunday Feb.5, 2006, God took Kenny home to be with him. He received his crown of glory.

All of us have a story and even as I write this, I can see your faces etched with sorrow, knowing that many of you have endured severe testing and trials and may be experiencing one at this very moment. Are you…

- Grieving the death of a loved one?
- Facing Insurmountable obstacles?
- Betrayed by a spouse or friend?
- Feeling helpless raising teenagers?
- Struggling with a marriage in crisis?
- Trapped in addictions?
- Praying for the salvation of loved ones?
- Saddened by a miscarriage or death of a baby?
- Caring for elderly and aging parents?
- Searching for employment?
- Dealing with a medical diagnosis?
- Other:_____

What do you do? How do you get through? How do you persevere and not give up? You question God and ask why? You often feel alone, frightened and inadequate to the task. And well-intentioned people give you pat answers and sage advice but cannot fathom the depth of your pain. There was only one place

I found the answers I needed and hopefully you will too. I'd like to invite you to come to that place with me today. Walk with me through the garden of Gethsemane. Gethsemane means "olive oil press." It is located at the foot of the Mount of Olives east of the city of Jerusalem. It is a relatively small garden. Actually, it's an orchard filled with olive trees, some believed to have been there in the time of Jesus. An olive tree grows slowly. The first seven years of its life it grows from 10 to 40 ft. in height. Between the months of April and June, small white perfume flowers appear in clumps on the branches. The olive tree only yields one olive to about 20 flowers andthe first sign of flowering takes 8 years. For a good harvest it will take 15 years. Olives are used for many things such as eating, healing, cooking, lighting, and anointing for kings. The garden of Gethsemane was a place of beauty and serenity, a secret place where Jesus could spend time alone to pray or teach his disciples. I had the wonderful experience of being in that garden and felt the peace and sacredness of the place. You'll get the same feeling for the place when you read Matt.26:36-46.

What is significant about the Garden of Gethsemane? Frequently we dwell on the Feast of Passover and the Crucifixion, but skim over the verses of Gethsemane. Yet we know its importance because it is recounted in all four of the gospels. Charles Spurgeon suggests that the passion actually began in Gethsemane. Jesus took his disciples to Gethsemane and told them to sit there while he went over to pray. When we find ourselves in Gethsemane, we need to invite our family and friends to be there for us also, praying and helping us in whatever way they are able. Kenny and I gratefully experienced the love from our family and church members. Jesus took Peter, James and John further into the garden with him, telling them that he was deeply troubled unto death. That's a time when you let only those closest to you know about your private pain. They understand that you are sorrowful and tearful, confused and exhausted. You ask them to watch and pray, because you know that you cannot make it through this struggle on your own strength. Jesus then goes a little further alone to pray to his Father. There's a holy place within us where we meet God, where only He knows the depth of our pain and anguish. Please understand that your loved ones will also sleep, not because they don't care, but because they are human. We can't begin to imagine Jesus' agony, even to the point of sweating great drops of blood. Jesus falls on his face and three times he prays,

"My Father, if it is possible, may this cup be taken from me,
yet not as I will, but as you will." Matt.26:39

The first lesson here demonstrates the tenderness and frailty of the human condition and the compassion of our God. Jesus prays three times. This encourages us to keep on praying and asking and persevering in prayer. The second lesson is even more important. It shows us the difference between submitting and embracing. To submit means to "subject oneself to" or to "give in to imposed conditions." It's often thought of in terms of punishment or discipline for people like prisoners, employees, and slaves. However, there are Christians who picture God as demanding and harsh. They are bound by legalism, hard and set rules and conditions. This is far from the truth of a believer who knows the reward of doing God's perfect will. To embrace means "to clasp, as in your arms, press to your heart, with joy and hope." The agony Jesus suffered in Gethsemane was not about the gruesomeness of physical pain, shame and ignominy, or even an attack from Satan. This was about taking the burden of all mankind's sins on himself and thus experiencing separation from his Father. Look intently at a cross. These are our sins taken and atoned for. We are forgiven and redeemed. He paid the price in full.

God's perfect will is EMBRACED in Gethsemane. Jesus didn't quit or give up because it was too hard. Jesus surrendered and embraced the Father's perfect will. It was then that something changed. We might call it a holy breakthrough.

"Who for the joy set before him endured the cross." Heb.12:2

Then God sent his ministering angels to Jesus. I remember experiencing these three stages of surrender. At first, I strongly resisted and fought against Kenny's diagnosis. I wept endlessly and begged God to take it away. Then, both of us submitted to God's will, still praying and believing in faith for a healing. God gave us *Dt.30:19-20* as our life verse to stand on. Every day, He sets before us life and death, and we chose life. Then came our surrender! We knew in our hearts that God was not going to heal Kenny physically here on earth but that his healing would be in eternity. He did heal him spiritually and brought about reconciliation within his family. Jesus clung to the Father's will with an affection that lifted him beyond all the sufferings that lay ahead. Kenny and I clung to the Father's will and were given unfathomable strength, peace and joy. Once we embraced the Father's will, we were able to walk into our destiny.

Not a single one of us is exempt from Gethsemane. The day and the hour will come when you are faced with a Gethsemane experience. And perhaps it will come more than once. Maybe you've already been there or maybe you're in the garden now. For some of you— it's still to come. This is not to generate fear and anxiety in us, but to reassure us that God is with us and will sustain us and send us His ministering angels.

We have three options in responding to our Gethsemane:

- Resist God's will.
- Submit to God's will.
- Surrender and embrace God's will.

If it is not embraced joyfully and obediently a hardness and bitterness sets in our hearts. Life loses it flavor and we become lifeless and dead. Can you even begin to imagine what your life would look like if you said **YES** to the Father's will in your Gethsemane?

- This is the place where you are changed.
- Where you come face to face with yourself and your vulnerabilities.
- Where you are pressed and crushed in order to walk into your destiny.
- Where you are given a glimpse into the heart of Christ.

Once you bow down in the garden and embrace God's will—something incredible happens. Jesus manifests himself to you and gives you exceeding great joy! It's then that …

- Marriages will be restored.
- Bondage to sin will be broken.
- Hope blossoms.
- Faith is strengthened.
- Perseverance is given.
- Grace is sufficient.
- Healing is given in the midst of pain.
- What seemed impossible is now possible.

- Testimony is given to the glory of God.
- Light will come out of darkness.
- The stone will be rolled away.
- He will wipe the tears from our eyes.
- He will turn our mourning into dancing.
- We will experience resurrection joy and power.

Daisy up Exercises:

Hold a cup or mug in your hands.

Look inside as if you are looking at your life right now.

What's in your cup today?

What are your struggles, worries, fears?

What is your Gethsemane?

Write it inside the mug below:

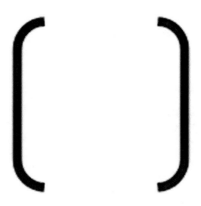

Read *Psalm 34*. Write out some of the verses that encourage you on 3 X 5 cards. Read them throughout the day and post them where you will often see them.

Journal Prompt:

What is the most difficult-the most pressing thing you are facing in your life today?

How is God asking you to respond? What does he want from you?

How do you feel about it?

How will you let go of your own will and embrace his will?

Prayer:

Hear my cry, O Lord, as I kneel in this Garden of Gethsemane. I am feeling hard-pressed and saddened in my present circumstances. Please strengthen me with your strong right hand and give me grace to face the day. I know you are with me in this midst of this trial. Please send your ministering angels to lift me up and keep my eyes focused on you. Let your face be ever before me. Amen.

Quote:

"All the world is full of suffering. It is also full of overcoming."
Helen Keller

DAY 23

DAISY UP...EMBRACING FORGIVENESS

"Forgive as the Lord has forgiven you."

Col.3:13

*J*une 6, 1944, the Allies invaded Normandy. General Eisenhower made the bold decision which became a major turning point in the war. That decision led to the eventual liberation of northern France from the Nazi Reich. It was a day that went down in history. It was a day of decision and deliverance. It took the defining courage of one man to make a bold and intrepid decision that led to victory.

How about you? Do you need to change something in your life? Do you need courage to make a bold and brave decision? Sometimes the hardest decision for anyone is to extend grace and forgiveness. That will be the focus and goal of our reflection today.

- To gain an understanding of forgiveness.
- To understand the effects of an unforgiving spirit.
- To understand the effects of forgiveness.
- To understand the steps to forgiveness.

Forgiveness is the act of setting someone free from an obligation to you that is the result of a wrong done against you or someone that you love. The act can be any hurtful thing. It's performed by a family member, spouse, friend, co-worker, neighbor, criminal, or stranger. In your mind, they become the enemy. They want to harm you, destroy your reputation, rejoice at your downfall, take unfair advantage of you, and make your life miserable. It's not a pretty picture, is it? Then you are commanded by the Word of God to forgive them. Often it's hard to forgive because we have a wrong understanding of forgiveness. Let's take a closer look at:

WHAT FORGIVENESS IS NOT:

- It is not approving of what they did to you or your loved ones.

    There was a woman caught in adultery (*John 8:9*).

Jesus did not approve of her sin. In fact, he told her to go and sin no more.

- It is not excusing what someone did against you. We do not cover their sins.

- It is not justifying what they did. Justify means to make right. What they did to you was wrong.

- It is not denying what they did. True forgiveness can only be offered after we come to terms with the reality of the situation.

- It is not forgetting what they did. We cannot forget meaningful or significant events in our lives whether positive or negative. We simply choose not to dwell on it or allow it to have power over us anymore.

- It is not reconciliation, because that requires the participation of two people. The other person may or may not want it. It's wonderful to seek it, however. But that does not mean you have to re-establish a close relationship or go to lunch with them. Sometimes it's best to terminate a relationship for the good of everyone concerned.

WHAT FORGIVENESS IS:

- It is being aware of what someone has done and still forgiving them anyway.

- It is keeping no record of wrongs. We don't file it away to bring up r bring up again and again.
- It is refusing to punish or seek revenge. We need to give up the human desire to see them get what they deserve. If we secretly long to see our enemies punished, we will eventually lose the anointing of the Spirit. Vengeance belongs to the Lord. Let it go.

"Do not take revenge my friends, but leave room for
God's wrath. It is mine to avenge; I will repay,
says the Lord." Ro.12:19

- It is not gossiping about what they did to others.

"Do not let any unwholesome talk come out of your mouths,
but only what is helpful for building others up according
to their needs, that it may benefit those
who listen." Eph.4:29

Anyone who truly forgives does not gossip about the offenders. This is often done with the intent to hurt some-one's reputation or good name.

That is beneath the love of a Christ follower and gains no respect.

- It is an inner condition of the Heart. Forgiveness must take place in the heart or else it is useless. Love is an intentional choice to forgive. If it's in our hearts, our words will show it. If there is bitterness it will eventually manifest itself in unpleasant ways.

This is why reconciliation is not essential. If I have truly forgiven someone in my heart but he or she still doesn't want to speak to me, I can still have inner peace. Unfortunately, many people we need to forgive don't even know they have done something wrong.

- It is an absence of bitterness.

"... and do not grieve the Holy Spirit of God. Get rid of all bitterness, rage and anger, brawling and slander, along with every form of malice." Eph.4:30

"See to it that no one misses the grace of God, and that no bitter root grows up to cause trouble and defile many."
Heb.12:15

How does bitterness manifest itself?

Temper tantrums.
High blood pressure.

Irritability.

Sleeplessness.

Obsession.

Getting even.

Depression.

Isolation.

Constant negativity.

Unforgiveness is like carrying a sack of potatoes around for a week. You can never put it down, thus it becomes heavy, burdensome, and smelly. Unforgiveness is like being in a prison cell except you are the keeper of the key. You have the power to let yourself out and choose life.

EFFECTS OF UNFORGIVENESS:

- Hinders our relationship with God.
- Slows our spiritual growth.
- Produces bitterness.
- Causes us anguish of soul.
- Makes us hard –hearted.
- Makes us proud and self-righteous.
- Makes us critical and judgmental.
- Holds us in captivity.
- Brings about physical illness.

- Leads to depression.
- Affects all my other relationships.

EFFECTS OF FORGIVENESS:

- Sets us free.
- Releases us from anguish.
- Transforms us in love.
- Fills our live with joy and peace.
- Restores our relationship with God and others.
- Clothes us with mercy and compassion.
- Opens us to the comforter—the Holy Spirit.
- Deepens our life of prayer.

After considering these lists, wouldn't you want to choose forgiveness? If you choose to forgive, here are some trustworthy steps to follow:

1. Acknowledge you have been hurt.
2. Surrender your right to get even.
3. Take the first step and ask God to help you.
4. Pray for those who hurt you.
5. Ask God to bless them.
6. Seek reconciliation if it seems wise and possible.

When you surrender unforgiveness to the Father, your life will be immediately transformed. You will feel lighter and the spirit of love will fill your whole being. It takes real courage and humility to grant forgiveness and extend the hand of grace. God will help you if you are willing. *"To forgive is the highest, most beautiful form of love. In return, you will receive untold peace and happiness." Robert Muller*

Daisy up Exercises:

Make a list of all the people you are not forgiving. Next to each name write how you were hurt and what you were feeling then and now. Next make a conscious decision to forgive them in Jesus' name. This is a decision…not a feeling. Ask God to heal you of any bitterness or hardness of heart. Let go of the desire to see them punished in any way. Give up any plan to seek revenge. Instead, ask God to bless them, their families, and circumstances.

Next, tear up your paper into tiny pieces and burn it in the fire. As the flame goes up, allow yourself to be totally set free. Let the peace of Christ fill your entire being. Give thanks to God for setting you free from the burden of unforgiveness. Now you can truly move forward in God's beautiful plan for your life.

Journal Prompt:

Write a letter to someone who has hurt you in the past or in the present. Tell them the whole situation from your perspective. Talk to them about your feelings and how this has affected your relationship. Ask their forgiveness if you had any part in the problem. Tell them you now forgive them and promise to pray for them and ask God to bless them. Sign it, but don't send it. Be as honest as you can and ask God to lift the burden from your shoulders. Let it go as you would a balloon into the air. Take a deep breath and feel God's peace within you.

Prayer:

Lord, you are the keeper of my heart and soul. I thank you that you have forgiven me all of my sins through the death of your son Jesus on the cross. Now I ask that I can share that same forgiveness with those who have hurt or offended me in any way. I want to be merciful and compassionate like you. Lift the burden of carrying this heavy weight of unforgiveness around with me. I now surrender it to you and ask you to replace it with your love and grace. I pray this in Jesus' name. Amen.

Quote:

"If you hate, you will give them your heart and mind." Nelson Mandela

DAY 24

DAISY UP…EMBRACING LOVE

"It is not rude, it is not self-seeking. It is not easily angered, it keeps no record of wrongs. 1 Co. 13:5

A few years ago, there was a television series titled, *CUPID*. It was idealistic and romantic. It centered around the search for love, finding that real love connection between two people. It spoke to the genuine need that all people have for real and lasting love in their lives. We all search for love, don't we? We may look in the wrong places and in the wrong way, but it is something every human being longs for. When I look around at our world, at all the sickness, loneliness, violence, crime, misery, broken homes and relationships, I ask myself, "What's missing?" The answer that comes to me is— *LOVE*. To love another person is the ultimate expression of love. And it takes a lifetime to learn about Love. One of the ways God builds your love is to test it. He tests it by putting you around irksome troublesome people. Here are four examples:

#1 DIFFICULT PEOPLE

- Cantankerous.
- Irresponsible.
- Immature.
- Cranky.
- Unruly.
- Irksome.
- Contrary.
- Perplexing.

#2 DEMANDING PEOPLE

- Have an agenda.
- Are aggressive.
- Get pushy.
- Are manipulating.
- Want things their own way.
- Can be stubborn.
- Are always right .
- Very self-centered.

- Demeaning.
- Expect perfection.

#3 DISAPPOINTING PEOPLE

- They are usually mean well.
- They will disappoint you and let you down.
- They are frustrating.
- They fail you in some way
- They may be betray you.
- They can be disloyal.

#4 DESTRUCTIVE PEOPLE

- They are hurtful intentionally.
- They are hateful.
- They are untrustworthy.
- They are deceitful.
- They are dangerous.
- They are disruptive.
- They are out to get you at any cost.

HOW DO I RESPOND TO THESE PEOPLE?

1 Co.13:5 counsels us with four ways to respond to these irksome, troublesome people in our lives.

FOUR MARKS OF AUTHENTIC LOVE

The first type are difficult people. There are many of these people in our lives. We need to learn how to deal with them in life situations. We also need to learn how to love them. You probably live or work with them on a daily basis. They can be very rude and obnoxious. What form of rudeness irritates you most?

Someone on their phone while at lunch with you?

Someone eating with their mouth open?

Someone driving below or above the speed limit?

Someone making marketing calls?

Someone who smirks at your remarks?

Other:_____

How do I respond in love to these difficult people?

Mark #1 LOVE IS NOT RUDE.

I must be tactful and not return their rudeness. Listen to them kindly and with patience. It may be that they have a valid point to make. Resist interrupting them or correcting them. If you listen lovingly, they will respond lovingly.

"Get rid of all bitterness, rage and anger, brawling and slander, along with every form of malice. Be kind and compassionate to one another forgiving each other, just as in Christ God forgave you." Eph.4:31

Rude people feel they are being authentic when they just blurt out what's on their mind without consideration of others. It results in hurt feelings and causes conflict. Rude people tend to focus on the negative rather than the positive. It's not what they say but how they say it. When words are spoken harshly, then the other person will become defensive. Be tactful, honest, and considerate. When you try to get even with somebody it puts you on the same level with them. When you return good for evil it puts you above them. Love is not rude.

Mark #2 LOVE DOES NOT DEMAND ITS OWN WAY.

I must learn to be understanding, and not demanding. Some people feel like they are entitled to something. They insist on their rights. They are pressing and wearisome. One of the greatest tests of character is how you treat the people who serve you. These are waitresses, flight attendants, gardeners, secretaries, postal carriers, store clerks, maids, and cleaners. Are you patient, kind, and considerate? The secret ingredient is **RESPECT.**

"Do nothing out of selfish ambition or van conceit, but in humility consider others better than yourselves. Each of you should look not only to your own interests, but also to the interests of others." Phil.2:3-4

The best place to begin is at home. Sometimes we're more polite to strangers than we are to the people we love. But the fruit of the Spirit it love, peace, patience, etc. There are two Greek words used for patience. One is *hupomone* which means patience with our circumstances. The other is *makromuthia* which means patience with people. *Makromuthia* is the one used in the fruit of the Spirit in *Gal. 5:22.* It is the supernatural outcome of being filled with the Holy Spirit. The more you try to understand people, the more patient you'll be with them. Try understanding their background, battles, and burdens. We don't know what is going on in their lives? Wouldn't you want to err more on the side of love? The people God places near us are not by accident. They are assigned to us by God. He may use them to complete His work in us. We think we'd be more content if they were out of our lives forever. God does have a sense of humor, doesn't he?

Mark #3 LOVE IS NOT IRRITABLE.

I must learn to be gentle not judgmental. There will always be people in your life who are going to disappoint you. Expect that your friends, family, parents, siblings, spouse, teachers, pastors, and even politicians will at times disappoint you. The reason is simple. Nobody is perfect. We are human beings with faults and failings. If you have to have a hard conversation with someone, the Bible tells us to do it gently, not harshly, not in a rude or mean way. It doesn't matter if you're right. If you're rude about it nobody's going to care what you have to say. They immediately get defensive. So treat others as you would like to be treated— respectfully.

"Therefore, let us stop passing judgment on each other."
Ro.14:12

"A gentle answer turns away wrath, but a harsh word stirs up anger." Prov.15:1

Choose your battles. Learn to cut each other some slack and be kind and gentle in your relationships. Change your attitude and your perspective because you will reap what you sow. Sow kindness and respect and that is what you will reap.

Mark #4 LOVE KEEPS NO RECORD OF WRONGS.

Don't repeat it, just delete it. This is the hardest lesson of all. How do you love people who intentionally want to hurt you, who are mean and haughty towards you? When people hurt us we have two natural tendencies. We will remember it and we will retaliate. We lock it up in our minds. We put it in our little black book. We never let them off the hook. We remember and rehearse it over and over again. We tell other people in order to get sympathy. Eventually, resentment builds a home in your mind and heart. This is a silent killer. Resentment turns to bitterness and it consumes you. Does this sound familiar? Are you feeling uncomfortable? Isn't there a kernel of truth here? The second thing we do is retaliate. We want to get even and make them pay. But God tells us not to keep a record of wrongs. How do I respond to people who have hurt me? How do I handle all those hurts, rejections, and wounds? You don't repeat it, you delete it. You erase it from your mind. Let it go. If you don't forgive, you only hurt yourself. It will slowly destroy you. Forgive and move forward with your life in Christ.

"He who covers over an offense promotes love." Prov.17:9

Daisy up Exercises:

Is there a difficult person in your life right now?
Is there a demanding person in your life right now?
Is there a disappointing person in your life right now?
Is there a destructive person in your life right now?

Draw a stick figure of them and write their name underneath. Then write all your feelings you have for them around the stick figure. Then write some of the verses from *1Co.13* under it. Imagine how you might apply these verses to this person.

Now:
Pray for them and ask God to bless them.
Think of a kind word you can speak to them.

Pay them a compliment with sincerity.

Give them a gift.

Do a kind deed for them.

Journal Prompt:

Write about a difficult unlovely in your life in story form. Create the character, plot, conflict, and resolution. Make it fictional and fun. This can be a very freeing exercise. Have fun with it. Humor always wins in the end.

Prayer:

Lord, teach me to love others as you love me. Show me how I can be a blessing in someone's life today…especially someone who rubs me the wrong way. I want to embrace the precepts of *1 Co.13*. It's easy to love my friends and family, but to show love to difficult and demanding people takes a lot of patience and strength of character. Help me to change the way I look at others and to respond in love no matter what happens. This is your command: to love one another. Help me to do it in Jesus name. Amen.

Quote:

"It is better to have loved and lost, than never to have loved at all."

Alfred Tennyson

DAY 25

DAISY UP…EMBRACING THE KINGDOM BUILDER

"What good is it for a man to gain the whole world,

yet forfeit his soul?"

Mark 8:36

*T*oday's reflection centers around the parable of the wise fool, whose also been dubbed the barn builder. We will examine the problems and consequences of **GREED**. In *Luke 12:13-15,* we observe a man asking Jesus to tell his brother to divide the inheritance with him. In ancient times it was quite common to go to a rabbi for a legal ruling such as this. The older brother usually received the double portion. How many times have you heard of families destroyed over fights and quarrels dealing with inheritance or the distribution of money and goods. But Jesus says in *Luke 12:15, "Watch Out! Be on* *your guard against all kinds of greed. A man's life does not consist in the abundance of his possessions."* In *v.16*, we see that Jesus refuses to mediate this issue. Instead, he tells a parable warning against all kinds of greed. The story Jesus tells disregards the man's rights and focuses on greed instead. The story does it indirectly as Jesus talks about a certain landowner. We conclude several things about him from this passage:

- Everything in his business is doing well.
- This year gave him an enormous bumper crop.
- He is very wealthy.

How many times have we said to ourselves, "Oh, if only I were rich, if only I'd win the lottery or inherit a lot of money." These thoughts breed envy and jealousy. In the play— Fiddler on the Roof— Tevye sings *If I Were a Rich Man* and he spells out all that he would do with his riches. That might prove to be an interesting exercise for all of us. In *Luke 12:17-19*, the rich farmer comes up with a plan. He ponders about what to do. His barns are too small to store up all the extra crops. Then he decides to build bigger barns to store all his abundant grain and goods. Then he can take it easy and enjoy his life for years to come.

What's wrong with this picture? You might say nothing. In fact, you may think he was wise to build a bigger barn so his crops wouldn't be wasted. You might call him perceptive, clever, wise, and discerning. You might even nominate him for Forbes Fortune 500. So what's wrong? This rich farmer didn't consider God and he didn't consider others. He even failed to thank God for his blessings. Also in those days, people lived in community with family and extended family; men gathered at the city gates and discussed all manner of things with each other. But this man seemed to be a loner. He lived alone not really thinking about or caring for anyone but himself. He was in control of his own life without any consideration of God.

In *Luke 12:20*, God called this man a fool. "*This very night your life will be demanded from you. Then who will get what you have prepared for yourself?*"

God called the rich man a fool because he was greedy. Greed is an excessive avarice or craving for such things as food, drink, wealth and possessions. Jesus does not say we should shun earthly riches, possessions or pleasures. But our life should not revolve around them either. Our theme song becomes more, more, more. We build bigger houses, bigger barns, gain more money, fame and fortune. But in the end, we can't take any of it with us.

There is a Jewish phrase, "*rich toward God*" which means giving to the poor. What will we take with us? We can only take what we have given to God and others. Death cannot take our gifts of love and gratitude from us because they have spiritual value. Life is not defined by what we own and possess. Store up treasure in heaven and be rich toward God. *"For where your treasure is, there your heart will be also." Matt.6:21*

The greed virus is in our bloodstream. We get the fever and runny nose of greed and it isn't long before we are building bigger barns. We quit thinking of wealth as something to be shared and we begin calculating it as power to be used. We think of it as something we control. We don't need others. We're reaping so much wealth that we need bigger barns. Building barns doesn't leave much energy left over for the kingdom work of loving our neighbors, let alone loving God. In America, it seems the main priority is to live the good life, to acquire money and wealth, and be included among the rich and famous. So this parable forces us to make a decision about what we want in this life. Do we want a life consumed with the things of this world? Do we want a life in close relationship with God? Do we want to display a life of mercy and compassion for others? Jesus is telling this man that the most important thing for him to do is not solve his problem but change his heart. How often have we asked God to change our situation or circumstances rather than our hearts?

"All day long he craves for more, but the righteous give without sparing." Prov.21:26

"Whoever loves money never has money enough; whoever loves wealth is never satisfied with his income. This too is meaningless." Ecc.5:10

But isn't this exactly what people think? Jesus warns us to be on our guard against all kinds of greed and covetousness… a grasping for more that is never satisfied or wanting more of what you already have. One's life does not consist in the abundance of his possessions but greed tells us otherwise.

What happens when our hearts are focused exclusively on ourselves?

FIVE PRINCIPLES:

#1 We do not acknowledge God for things He has done for us. Luke 12:16

The rich man in the parable was a farmer but he represents all human beings who are led astray by all kinds of greed. As this farmer looked at his amazing harvest he did not see the hand of God. He saw only his own effort and hard work. He was a man who possessed much and expected more.

#2 We make plans without considering God and others. Luke 12:17-18

There is no thought of sharing his goods and possessions with others, especially the less fortunate. The landowner was not attentive to God.

#3 We envision taking life easy. v.19

We control the fate of our money and investments expanding. *James 4* tells us that we do not know what will happen tomorrow. The Word of God does not discourage us from looking to the future with great hope and anticipation, but we need to realize that God is ultimately in charge. He doesn't want us to fixate only on our own ease and pleasure.

#4 We store our treasure in the wrong places. v.20

The word "fool" in biblical language was not about mental ability but about spiritual discernment. In scripture a fool is a man who leaves God out of the picture.

"The fool says in his heart; there is no God." Ps.14:1

The landowner lived his life as if God didn't exist. He didn't understand that his material blessings came from God. He thought only of his gold, money, and possessions, instead of God. He chose pleasure over people. He gave himself over to ease instead of eternity. He was a fool because he forgot about God and eternity.

"What good is it for a man to gain the whole word,
yet forfeit his soul?" Mark 8:36

The biggest fool is not the one who doesn't believe in a God; it is the one who believes, but lives as if God did not exist. To be a fool is to have missed your purpose in this life. The truth of the matter is—you cannot take any of it with you. So there is no need to wear yourself out accumulating it. Whatever you have is yours now to use, but one day it will be taken from you and you will stand before the Lord and give an account of how you used it.

5. We will find ourselves in conflict with God's plan for our lives. Luke 12:21

The fool lays up treasure for himself and is not rich toward God. Riches in this world have one major shortcoming, they do not have purchasing power after death. On the other hand, "*riches toward God*" do have purchasing power after death because they are used to bless others.

Often our wealth isolates us from the real problems of the world. The cry of the poor and destitute can't even reach our ears. I don't want to be like the wise fool and not have a clue about the desperate cry of the brokenhearted, do you? Parables like this can scare us, so that we end up trying to justify our lives rather than admitting we need to change our lives. Did you know this is the only parable where God actually shows up on the scene? What if God showed up on the scene of my life today? What would he call me? A Barn Builder or a Kingdom Builder.

How do we become rich toward God?

- Invest in your relationship with God.
- Invest in His church.
- Invest in the lives of the poor and needy.
- Invest in building disciples for Christ.

Let's stop justifying our indulgences and just call them what they are—selfish pleasures. Let's ask God to forgive us when we tend to fill our own cupboards rather than the pantries of the poor. Let's ask God's forgiveness when we build our own kingdom rather than partnering with Habitat for Humanity or some other organization that helps the less fortunate. Let's ask forgiveness for not caring enough and ask God to help us care more. Let's ask forgiveness for choosing to look out for ourselves instead of others—for organizing our lives in such a way that the cry of the poor fades in the dark of night. Let's commit ourselves to grow "*rich toward God*" beginning today!

Daisy up Exercises:

Make a sketch of 2 barns: Label one "Rich toward Myself" and label the other "Rich toward God." Now write or cut out words and pictures from magazines that illustrate how you make yourself rich. When you are finished, do the same thing in the second barn showing how you are rich toward God.

When you are finished… mark an X through the one you want to let go of and write the words I CHOOSE THIS under the barn you want to commit yourself to.

Now choose a charity or poor family, widows, elderly or shut-ins, soup kitchen, shelter, or school that you can help with your resources. Inquire how you can help them? Then be intentional and write your act of kindness in the space below:

Journal Prompt:

Write your own prayer or words of commitment to God.

Prayer:

Father God, I thank you for all the blessings in my life. I am profoundly grateful that you have provided for me and my family. I don't want to keep it all my blessings for myself, Lord. Please show me the best way that I can become a Kingdom builder. I want to be a good steward of all that you have given to me. Show me whom to bless and how I am to do it. Increase my love for your people and use me to touch others' lives in meaningful ways. I pray this in Jesus name. Amen.

Quote:

"Greed is a nearly invisible sin, a tiny parasite that makes its home in the intestine of wealth." Eugene Peterson

DAY 26

DAISY UP…EMBRACING SECURITY IN GOD

"May those who love you be secure."

Ps.122:6

*W*e live in a time when insecurity is plaguing our nation and our world. People are insecure not only in this economy, but in almost every area of their lives. When we look at history, we were just recovering from World War I in 1919. Then the 1920's became a time of great prosperity in America. There were great advances in technology— cars, stock exchange, songs about the good times and blue skies. It was so good that Hoover in his pre-election speech said, *"Poverty will be banished from this nation."*

All this came to an end in 1929 when the stock market crashed. America entered what historians called the Great

Depression. It lasted a decade. Thousands of people went bankrupt, employees were let go, consumer demands plummeted, and people lived in cardboard huts called Hoover Ville. Men wore tattered clothing and people committed suicide. We learn that history repeats itself and human folly and greed rise to the surface again and again. People find security in their homes, possessions, status, money, friends, careers, jobs, degrees, home security systems, locks, bolts, police, organizations, churches and God.

What does security mean to you? What makes you feel secure? Jot down some of your thoughts in the space below:

Webster's dictionary defines security as: The quality or state of being secure; freedom from danger, fear or anxiety. And in Maslow's hierarchy of needs—security ranks as number two. Many of you reading this today may be dealing with issues of insecurity in various forms. We desperately long to find security in these ways:

WHO?

relationships	teachers	spouses	family
friends	co-workers	pastors	neighbors

WHAT AND WHERE?

homes	possessions	knowledge
careers	degrees	jobs
money	purpose	approval
status	reputation	justice system
popularity	economy	church
country	schools	investment

WHEN?

We look for security each and every day.

WHY?

We don't want to be dependent on others. We don't want to be vulnerable and needy. We don't want to be indebted to others. We don't want to change our lifestyle or be lacking in any way. We don't always need to be rich, but we do want to be secure. When we find ourselves feeling insecure we can walk down paths we wouldn't normally take. We might find ourselves falling into addictions, depression, illness, isolation, dishonesty, and withdrawal from God and the church.

We find ourselves calling out to God and asking…

- When will this be over?
- When will I have some peace?
- When will things get back to normal?
- When will I feel safe and secure again?
- When will I know?
- When will I get a job?
- When will my house sell?
- When will I be able to pay my bills?
- When will I get health benefits?

"I cried out to God for help; I cried out to God to hear me."
Ps.77:1

Let's look at this topic in the light of the Trinity—Father, Son, and Holy Spirit.

#1 We are secure in the Father's Love

During my childhood I remember that we were sometimes insecure and lacking in our basic needs, struggling to stay afloat. But my greatest security was in the love of my father and mother. For me that was enough. I felt safe and secure because I trusted them and knew they would take care of me.

As believers, the same is true of our God and Father…

His love endures forever.

His love is everlasting.

He has manifested his wonderful love in my life.

He directs his love towards me.

For great is his love toward me.

He is my everlasting Father.

He is my creator.

He is the potter and I am the clay.

He is my fortress and my deliverer.

He is my rock, my refuge and my strength.

He is my place of mercy.

He watches over me day and night.

He hears my cry for help and answers me.

He reaches down and pulls me out of the pit.

He is faithful even when I am faithless.

He is my comforter and provider.

He is my healer.

In *Dt.7:6*, God calls me his treasured possession. A possession is something acquired. The word literally means "to walk around" referring to the ancient practice of acquiring a piece of property. Walking around a section of land denoted ownership. God has walked around us. He has claimed us as his possession.

"May those who love you be secure." Ps.122:6

The greatest sign of the Father's Love is in *John 3:16, "For God so loved the world that He gave his one and only Son, that whoever believes in him shall not perish but have eternal life."*

"I will maintain my love to him forever, and my covenant with him will never fail." Ps.89:28

Write in the space below: I am secure in the Father's love.

```


```

#2 We are secure in Jesus

In *Eph.1:11* Paul tells us that we were chosen in Christ. This is referring to those Jews who like Paul had become believers before many Gentiles had. Then he goes on to say in *Eph.1:13-14, "And you also were included in Christ when you heard the word of truth, the gospel of salvation. Having believed, you were marked in him with a seal, the promised Holy Spirit, who is a deposit guaranteeing our inheritance until the redemption of those who are God's possession—to the praise of His glory."*

Your real security is your identity in Christ. You are secure in your position as God's sons and daughters. You are accepted by the Father because you are in Christ Jesus. *Matt.10:32, "Whoever acknowledges me before men, I will also acknowledge him before my Father in heaven."* You are secure in Christ because of His suffering, death, and resurrection. You are secure in Christ because you have been saved, redeemed, forgiven and reconciled to the Father. You are secure in Christ because...

- He is the way, the truth, and the life.
- He is the bread of life.
- He is the light of the world.
- He is our savior and shepherd.
- He is the vine and we are the branches.
- He is the Lamb of God.
- He is the son of the Most High.
- He is the root of Jesse.
- He is the image of the invisible God.
- He is our redeemer.
- He is our healer.
- He is our bridegroom.
- He is our life.
- He is our friend.

Having believed, confessed and repented of our sin, and accepted Jesus as Lord and Savior of our lives. Write in the space below: I am secure in Jesus.

#3 We are secure in the Holy Spirit

Let me go back to another definition of security by Webster. It is something given; deposited or pledged to make certain. A document proving evidence of ownership. Recall *Eph.1:13*, *"…having believed, you were marked in him with a seal, the promised Holy Spirit, who is a deposit guaranteeing our inheritance."* In those days a seal denoted ownership and security. To seal something was to make it certain; to promise that it was true and binding as when a man seals a deed or last will and testament. Any document of the king or under his authority was marked with a seal…his royal insignia was stamped in the warm liquid of wax, and it would quickly harden into a seal. The seal could be opened only by the one to whom it was sent or under the direct authority of the king. Nothing and no one on earth or in the heavens has the authority or power to break God's seal.

We are saved for Christ alone. The Greek word for deposit is *arrabon*—a legal term meaning first installment or down payment. A commitment that full purchase would occur later. So we are very secure, sealed with the Holy Spirit who is the deposit insuring our inheritance. Jesus didn't leave us orphans, He sent us His Holy Spirit.

The Spirit of Truth.

Counselor and Comforter.

Breath of the Almighty.

Spirit of Christ.

Spirit of grace.

Spirit of adoption.

Spirit of understanding.

Spirit of wisdom.

Spirit of wind and fire.

Spirit of the living God.

Spirit of love.

Write in the space below: I am secure in the Holy Spirit.

Paul says that when we are weak then we are strong. I believe the same is true with security. When I am insecure, then I am secure in God. I no longer have to depend on myself but on God. I can finally let go and let God. Don't you want to be able to stand up today and say with confidence :

I am secure in my Father's love.
I am secure in my Lord and Savior Jesus Christ.
I am secure and sealed with His Holy Spirit.
God is asking us to trust in Him and believe that we are secure in him.

"Let the beloved of the Lord rest secure in Him, for He shields him all day long and the one the Lord loves rests between his shoulders." Dt.33:12

God is asking you to trust Him today-not tomorrow-TNT. It's not when you get your job, not when your relationships are fixed, not when you are healed, or your troubles are over. He wants us to know that whatever is going on in our lives right now—we are safe and secure in Him. He will never abandon or forsake us. He is our God and nothing is too hard for him. His arm is not too short to save. He is the Great I Am!

Daisy up Exercises:

Take a moment…close your eyes and quiet your spirit. Answer this question: Where am I feeling most insecure right now?

Write it down on your card below:

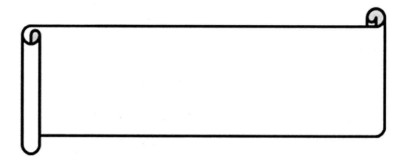

Pray this prayer out loud. Lord, I surrender to you today, this area of my greatest insecurity. Help me to trust in your unfailing love and provision.

Journal Prompt:

Read Jeremiah 18:1-6

Draw a pottery object and imagine it is you. What does it mean that God is the potter and you are the clay? What is he molding in your life right now? Are you resisting the hand of the potter? How? What can you do to allow yourself to be molded in the Potter's Hand? Why will you feel secure in the potter's hand?

Write a haiku poem about the potter and the clay. The first line contains 5 syllables, the second line contains 7 syllables, and the third line 5 syllables.

Here's a sample: *Your poem:*

In the hollow of
the potter's hand I am held
in exquisite love

Prayer:

I thank you, Father, that I am secure in your love. You constantly watch over me and guide my steps along your path. I know that if I walk with you, I have all I need in life. But if I am not with you, I am lonely and insecure. You are all that I need. You will provide for me and my family in every area of our lives because we trust in you. Thank you, Father, for the peace of knowing I am secure in your love and that you will guard and protect me all of my life. All honor be yours. Amen.

Quote:

"Where does your security lie? Is God your refuge, your hiding place, your stronghold, your shepherd, your counselor, your friend, your redeemer, your savior, your Guide? If He is, you don't need to search any further for security." Elisabeth Elliot

DAY 27

DAISY UP…EMBRACING GOD'S GRACE

"The grace of God is with you no matter what happens."

1 Pe.5:12

Have you ever felt stuck and in a rut? Have you felt like you can't move forward? Have you wondered if there was a light at the end of the tunnel? Have you cried out to God asking how long, O Lord? If your answer is yes, then take comfort because you are not alone. Even those who appear to have the perfect life, will find themselves in a rut once in a while. It's part of the human condition that confronts all of us at one time or another. The psalms are indicative of the longing of God's people.

"I am worn out from groaning; all night long I flood my bed with weeping and drench my couch with tears." Ps.6:6

"How long, O Lord? Will you forget me forever?" Ps.13:1

"How long must I wrestle with my thoughts, and every day have sorrow in my heart?" Ps.13:2

"Record my lament; list my tears on your scroll, are they not in your record?" Ps.56:8

"Day and night I cry out before you." Ps.88:1

"I have had enough, Lord….I'm all alone." 1 Kings 19:4

God tells Elijah in *1 Kings* that he is not alone. There are 7000 others who have not bowed their knees to Baal. Sometimes when we feel all alone, isolated and cut off, it helps to know there are others struggling also.

Let's take a personal survey: (place a check before those that apply to you)

- Praying for a job for a long time.
- Praying for a loved one to know Jesus.

- Praying for healing from sickness.
- Praying for a different decision.
- Praying for God to change your circumstances.
- Praying for your marriage.
- Praying for forgiveness and reconciliation.
- Praying for your finances to improve.
- Praying for guidance in a situation.
- Praying for your children to turn around.
- Praying for courage to do the right thing.
- Praying for God to bring the right soul mate into your life.
- Praying for deliverance from an addiction.
- Praying for an end to grieving and loss.
- Praying for provision.

If you were to compare your list with another's, you would discover that you are not alone. That's why I want to talk with you about God's Sustaining Grace, especially in times when you're ready to give up hope.

"Let us then approach the throne of grace with confidence,
so that we may receive mercy and find grace to help us in
our time of need." Heb.4:16

God doesn't just want to save us. He wants to sustain us in the journey!

Recently, our women's Bible Study Group completed a study by Priscilla Shirer called One in a Million. She talks about the Israelites deliverance from bondage in Egypt and their journey to the Promised Land which was 150 miles less than a month's journey. But God was not in a hurry so He purposely led them into the wilderness. Why would God do that? The answer is fairly simple: they weren't ready for military battle and if they went the shorter route they would have been destroyed. He also wanted to use that wilderness time to draw them closer to Him.

When we are in the wilderness, the in-between places, understand that God has a purpose. We may not understand it, but we know God and his character. We can trust that he is faithful and will always act in our best interests. These are the times you hold on to his sustaining grace. This is the grace that empowers you to keep on going when you feel like quitting and giving up. It is the power to grasp hold of God's hand and not let go—no matter what happens.

There are three things that cause us to give up and let go of God's hand. These are the things that make us lose our grip.

#1 TEMPTATION

"No temptation has seized you except what is common to man. And God is faithful; He will not let you be tempted beyond what you can bear. But when you are tempted,

He will also provide a way out so that you can stand up under it." 1Co.10:13

Temptations are designed by the devil to do two things:

- To lead us into sin.
- To turn us away from God.

No one is exempt from temptation because they are common to man. We need to remember that it's not a sin to be tempted but it is a sin to give in to temptation and act on it. What can we do?

- Ready yourself.

   Temptation can come in like a roaring lion or like a thief in the night. It comes when we are unaware, discouraged, vulnerable, or depressed. Opportunity knocks only once but temptation keeps banging at our door.

- Resist the evil one.

   The Word of God tells us to stand firm. That means to be steadfast. We can't negotiate, waver, or move back and forth between God's camp and the devil's camp. Resist the voice of the enemy.

- Refocus your mind.

    When tempted, you need to walk away. Change your thoughts and your attitudes. It's like switching your radio dials. Go to God's Word, put on praise music, or do a kind deed for someone in need.

#2 TIREDNESS

"Come to me all you who are weary and burdened, and I will give you rest. Matt.11:28

We know only too well that life can be exhausting. It takes a lot of energy to get up in the morning and face the day. You may have children who are demanding much of your time and attention, there's work, cleaning, cooking, car-pooling, church, volunteering, family celebrations and friend get-togethers. It seems everybody wants a piece of you. That's when the devil creeps in and tells you to just let go. He makes you feel bruised and battered and all alone. It's in those times that we can make some foolish decisions that we later regret. That's when you turn away from the devil and turn toward God. You can be confident that He is waiting to show you mercy and give you rest under the shelter of his wings. Simplify your life. Stop struggling and start trusting your heavenly Father.

#3 TROUBLED

"The Lord is close to the brokenhearted and saves those who are crushed in spirit." Ps.34:18

We don't like to hear it, but there aren't many quick fixes and easy solutions to our problems. They are often unplanned, unrelenting, and undeserved. The most difficult are the ones that are unfair and long term. If it's two months or even a year, we can accept it and prepare ourselves to get through it. We build up our adrenalin, our faith, our resources, and charge ahead. But when it drags on and on with no end in sight, we begin to lose steam and peter out. Strangely, that's when God is closest to us, aware of our every thought and need.

"But this happened that we might not rely on ourselves but on God who raises the dead." 2 Co. 1:19

This is the time to stop the *if only* game and fix our gaze on Christ. As Anne Graham Lotz says so beautifully, "Just give me Jesus."

What do you do when you can't fix the problem, solve it, or control it? You wish that you could wave a magic wand and erase it. It's difficult to feel so powerless. But this is the time you pour out your heart to God.

"Trust in Him at all times, pour out your hearts to him, for God is our refuge." Ps.62:8

You grasp hold of God's hand and hold on to His sustaining grace! Grace can mean this—

G rasp hold of God's hand and hang on.

R ead His Word and rely on Him.

A ccept His will, stop resisting, and surrender.

C ount your blessings.

E xpect a breakthrough.

WHERE DO YOU NEED GOD'S SUSTAINING GRACE TODAY?

"I begged the Lord three times to take this problem away from me. But he said, my grace is sufficient for you for my power is made perfect in weakness." 2 Co.12:9

This was Paul's breakthrough. Now it's time for your breakthrough. The most important thing to remember is this: It's really not about your circumstances but how you respond to them. It will make all the difference in how you move through your trials to transformation. Hold out your hand to God and take hold of his sustaining Grace.

Daisy up Exercises:

A prophetic action is more than a spoken word of prophecy or word of knowledge. It is an action, something we DO under the anointing of the Holy Spirit as an act of obedience to release the power, the presence and the victory of God into a situation.

Write your trial or struggle on a 3 x5 card and attach it to a rope. Lay the rope across the floor, preferably in your prayer space. Take a step of faith and walk over the rope. When you step over this line you are saying that you believe God for your breakthrough and that you are willing to hold on to His sustaining grace till that happens. This is a prophetic action. Believe that God will honor it.

Do your own acrostic for GRACE

G

R

A

C

E

Journal Prompt:

Pray the serenity prayer below and copy it in your journal.

God grant me the serenity to accept the things I cannot change, courage to change the things I can and wisdom to know the difference.

What do you need to accept at this time in your life?

What are the things you can't change right now?

What are the things you can change?

Prayer:

Lord, I know that your grace surrounds me and fills me. It is your gift to me as I walk my journey on this earth. I know there have been times when I've lost hope, turned away from you, given up on you, and made some bad decisions. Today, I want to change all of that. I purposely reach up to take hold of your hand and I promise to not let go. I'm going to trust you with every aspect of my life and I'm going to keep my eyes fixed on you. Your Presence is always with me filling me up and strengthening me. Thank you for your Grace, Lord!

Quote:

"That is the mystery of grace: it never comes too late." Francois Mauriac

DAISY UP...EMBRACE THE REPAIRER OF CRACKS

"....and do not give the devil a foothold."

Eph.4:27

*D*o you remember a somewhat superstitious practice of walking down the street and avoiding the cracks? They told me it was bad luck to step on a crack. I never took it seriously, since it was more of a game. But as I grew older, I realized that I definitely needed to watch out for cracks –not on the sidewalks- but in my life.

Cracks are openings, gaps, rips, breaches, clefts, or breaks. When we first moved into our house, my husband noticed some cracks in the front steps that he wanted fixed. Cracks can be dangerous, foundations can crumble and creatures can creep inside your home.

Let me share an incredible but true story about a large crack that changed a city's destiny. It was the city of Sardis which was a place of magnificence, luxury, and unlimited wealth. It sat on a natural acropolis. Three sides were sheer perpendicular rock 1500 feet above the valley. The fourth side had a softer slope protected by the city wall and gate. This city was invincible and impenetrable. King Cyrus of Persia had tried several times to get into the city without success and offered a handsome reward to any soldier who could find a way. It took place during a time of battle. One of the king's soldiers noticed the rock on which Sardis stood had cracks and faults in it. At one point, one of the soldiers in Sardis dropped his helmet off the edge and made his way down what appeared to be a crack below the wall, emerged outside, retrieved his helmet, and disappeared back inside. The Persian soldier reasoned that there must be a crack large enough to let a man through the wall. The next night the Persian army climbed through the crack and found the city unguarded with the soldiers asleep. Can you imagine the reaction of the people when they found their invincible city taken over by the enemy? They were stunned and unbelieving. What happened? The people became complacent, lazy, apathetic, and smug. They didn't fix the cracks in their structure. And would you believe that years later history repeated itself. Once again the city was captured by soldiers creeping up the steep cliffs through a crack to sleeping soldiers. Amazing isn't it? They didn't learn their lesson the first time.

You may wonder what this story has to do with you. Consider that what happened to Sardis can also happen to you in the spiritual realm. When was the last time you checked for cracks in your life, character, or behaviors? These cracks may start out small but we know how they grow and widen big enough for the enemy to get through.

"…and do not give the devil a foothold." Eph.4:27

Some of these cracks are thrust upon us or can be traced to a painful event in our past. Some of these cracks come about because of our neglect, apathy, or mediocre attitude toward sin.

WHAT DO THESE CRACKS LOOK LIKE?

Accidents.

Depression.

Childhood abuse.

Job loss.

Disability.

Cutting yourself.

Eating disorders.

Sexual immorality.

Bad companions.

Rebellion.

Selfishness.

Greed.

Envy and Jealousy.

Pride.

Robert McGee identifies 4 false beliefs or cracks that Satan uses to undermine our sense of worth. You may see yourself in several but one is usually more prominent. We need to prayerfully replace the lie with God's truth so that we can repair that crack or fault line. Satan uses these cracks to widen the gap between us and God.

THE FOUR FALSE BELIEFS:

Performance

Approval

Blame

Shame

We all have cracks and faults in our character simply because we are human. So what are we going to do about them? First ,listen to the Word of God.

"Be self-controlled and alert. Your enemy the devil prowls around like a roaring lion looking for someone to devour."
1Pe.5:8

Second, allow God to expose the cracks in your character. You can't fix what you do not acknowledge. A hidden crack can be exposed that I don't want anyone to know about. But when it is acknowledged and revealed the lie is broken. Jesus exposed people- not to humiliate them- but to alert them to danger and show them the way to get back on track. He hated the Pharisees' hypocrisy; he was sad that the rich young man loved money more; he rebuked Martha's anxiety; he told the woman caught in adultery to go and sin no more; he chastised the people in his hometown for their unbelief. We have a Jesus who is able to redeem our darkest moments and deepest fears, if we give him access to our hearts. Let me share Shanna's testimony from the house of hope. She was raped at age 5; introduced to porn at age 7; given drugs at age 9; and became pregnant at age 12 having an abortion to fix the problem. All this led to depression, cutting, and attempted suicide. She went through drug rehab and counseling, but nothing seemed to help. When Shanna was asked about getting to know Jesus, she said, "You gotta be kidding." But when she met Jesus, her life changed radically. She called herself a born again virgin. She was gifted with an amazing singing voice which brought hope to others.

Jesus became the repairer of her cracks. He can be the repairer of yours too.

JESUS, the Repairer of Cracks, is the only one to whom we can go.
He has already redeemed you.
Fixes what is broken in you.
Delivers, heals, and forgives you.
Takes away your shame.
Restores your worth.
Revives your soul.
Gives you a new life and a second chance.

In place of the cracks, Jesus has become our solid rock, a sturdy our foundation.

"He alone is my rock and my salvation; he is my fortress,
I will never be shaken." Ps.62:2

He wants to repair those cracks.
He wants to make you whole.
He wants to give you a second chance.
He wants to make you whole again.

Will you come to him? He's waiting for you with unfailing love and compassion.

Daisy up Exercises:

Draw a retaining wall with several cracks in it. On each crack, write an area that you need to work on—an area where you have become lax. Then draw another retaining wall with no cracks. Write all over the wall words of encouragement, victory, praise, and love. Choose this conquering wall and put it on display.

Journal Prompt:

Write a letter to your best friend telling him/her about the cracks in your wall. Ask them for advice on filling in the cracks. What would they say? Be honest and open in this exercise. How would you respond to them? End by thanking them and asking them for prayer. This can be a freeing exercise. Don't think too much—just write, write, write. You will be amazed.

Prayer:

Father, I know that I have a lot of cracks in my wall and I want to look at them honestly today. I want to list them without condemnation or guilt. I just want to be able to acknowledge them and then ask for your help and grace to fix them. I know it won't be an easy task but you've promised to heal and restore me. Thank you for trustworthy friends who can pray for me and encourage me to repair the cracks in my foundation. I'm taking a stand and I choose Jesus as my rock and my foundation. I pray this in His name. Amen.

Quote:

"There's a crack (or cracks) in everyone…that's how the light of God gets in."
—Elizabeth Gilbert

DAY 29

DAISY UP...EMBRACING REAL POWER

*"My grace is sufficient for you, for my power
is made perfect in weakness."*
2 Co.12:9

few years ago, Mattie Stepanek was on the Oprah show. He was a young boy with a rare form of muscular dystrophy. He lost a sister and two brothers from the same disease and his mother had it in the adult form. At the age of three, Mattie began writing poetry to help himself deal with the loss of his brother. He had three wishes in life: To meet Oprah Winfrey, Jimmy Carter, and to publish his poetry. He accomplished all three before he died just one month before his fourteenth birthday. Mattie was especially known as a peace advocate. Despite all his setbacks, this young boy possessed real power.

Shortly after that Oprah show, I saw a clip of a woman who had stage four cancer. But this amazing woman didn't allow this diagnosis to kill her. Instead, it was pushing her to live her life to the fullest. She possessed real power.

Then, I saw a program with Randy Pausch. He was a professor at Carnegie Mellon University in Pittsburgh, Pennsylvania. He was diagnosed with pancreatic cancer. This man became famous for his *Last Lecture* which was featured on television and became a book on the best seller list. He said, *"When you come to the end of your time, you don't look at what you did in life, but what you didn't do."* His life and his fight inspired thousands of people everywhere. That's real power.

Lastly, my husband, Kenny Moore, lived humbly and died victoriously. His journey through ALS- Lou Gehrig's Disease- will always be etched in my mind as a journey through Grace. He had to depend on others for absolutely everything. There was no place for pride or self-sufficiency. Yet, in his weakness, he possessed real power.

"My grace is sufficient for you, for my power is made perfect in weakness." 2Co.12:9

This is a passage where Paul describes a fierce struggle in his life over which he has no power. He asks God three times to remove it but God tells him that His grace is sufficient for him.

What about you? Do you need to hear that from God today? Have you ever felt utterly powerless in your life?

- Maybe you're dealing with a habit or addiction that you feel powerless to break.
- Maybe a relationship is becoming toxic.
- Maybe problems are escalating at work.
- Maybe you're stuck in a rut and can't find your way out.
- Maybe you're feeling powerless to pay bills and provide for your family.
- Maybe you've been given a fatal or serious diagnosis.
- Maybe your home and all your possessions have been destroyed by fire.

No matter what your situation may be, would you agree that at some time in our lives we feel powerless? Those are the times we call on God and cry out for help. The good news is that God does not want us to live powerless or defeated lives.

"For God did not give us a spirit of timidity, but of power, of love, and self-discipline." 2Tim.1:7

WHERE DO WE GET THIS POWER?

Let's imagine a Harley Davidson motorcycle. If I tried to push it around a race track, over hills, and around curves and berms without tapping into the engine's power, you'd think I was crazy. Wouldn't you? I've watched some motocross races on video. I've observed that the action is –

faster, faster, faster

tough turns

sharp curves

ruts and grooves

bumps and hills

extreme jumps

dangerous crashes

These riders don't ask, "What if I fail?" They ask, "What if I win?" They know failures and mistakes are just a part of life. Anyone who's ever succeeded has failed at some point and learned from their mistakes. But they kept trying till they got it right. These are the real champions and heroes in everyday life.

God has a word for you today. Maybe you're feeling power-less in a situation.

Perhaps you want to quit and give up. Maybe you're wondering how you got back to this place? People will say, "Pick yourself up, dust yourself off, and start all over again." It's easier said than done, isn't it?

HOW DO I DO THAT?

You kick start and rev up the engine. You tap into God's power for your life.

"Some trust in chariots and some in horses, but we trust in the name of the Lord our God." Ps.20:7

This incredible power is available to all of us. In our lives, in our marriages, in our families, in our work, in our relationships, in achieving our dreams and goals.

The paradox is that we are given this power by learning humbly. Humble means to lie low; to make yourself flat; to put yourself under. There's a man in the Bible who took a hard crash, yet God gave him the power to begin again. His name was Simon Peter. Peter and each of us who "learn humbly" go through three stages.

First stage: the call

Simon was one of the original members of Christ's racing team. Jesus changed his name to Peter, which means rock.

Jesus told him that he was the team captain and champion and that he was going to build a brand new team around him. Peter realized this was an honor and responsibility.

Second stage: the wall

Like many of us, Peter becomes over-confident. He vowed that he'd never deny Christ. But on the night before the big race, he crashed and denied Christ not once but three times. He lost his courage and became very afraid.

Third stage: the fall

In *Luke 22:61*, Jesus turned and looked straight at Peter. In that gaze, Peter remembered his promise. The Bible tells us that Peter went out and wept bitterly. He was a broken man at this point knowing that he betrayed Christ. Jesus didn't say a word, didn't reprove him, just looked at him with compassion. Jesus looked straight into Peter's heart and saw the regret, the guilt, the shame. Christ gave Peter a second chance. Peter learned humbly and received real power to begin again.

Just like he did with Peter, Jesus is looking straight into your eyes. He sees your heart, and he looks at you with compassion, not judgment. He wants to bless you and your future. He still has a plan and a divine purpose for your life.

Where do we learn humbly? Where do we tap into God's power?

AT THE FOOT OF THE CROSS

"I want to know Christ and the power of his resurrection."

Phil.3:10

Today some of you, like Peter …

Are dealing with guilt and shame.

Are filled with many regrets.

Are alienated from Christ.

Are broken-hearted and crushed in spirit.

Are held captive – powerless over some sin in your life.

Are holding deep resentment and bitterness in your heart.

Are struggling with health issues.

Are depressed and discouraged.

Are anxious and fearful.

Are dealing with trouble in your marriages.

Jesus is about bringing things back to life. Jesus is about bringing people back to life. And it can happen for you also at the foot of the cross.

You can be healed.

You can be forgiven.

You can be restored.

You can be set free.

Your crooked ways can be set straight.

You can be given a new start.

You can learn humbly.

You can dream again.

You can receive life.

You can find peace.

Your real power begins when you come humbly before Jesus on the cross.

Daisy up Exercises:

Be still and quietly pour your heart out to God.
Tell him where you need his power in your life.
Ask him for grace and humility to begin again.

Go to You-tube and watch videos about Mattie Stepanek and Randy Pausch.

Journal Prompt:

Finish this acrostic:

R

E

A

L

P

O

W

E

R

Describe what this means to you in one sentence. What is it you want to ask of God your Father after writing this acrostic?

Prayer:

Father God, I want your resurrection power in my life. I need your strength and courage to move forward. Please forgive me my sins, heal me, and restore me. I know your grace is enough for me. I want to be able to move in your power and strength.

I want to live a life pleasing to you in every way. Hear my prayer in Jesus name. Amen.

Quote:

"Always continue the climb. It is possible for you to do whatever you choose, if you first get to know who you are and are willing to work with a power that is greater than ourselves to do it."
Ella Wheeler Wilcox

DAY 30

DAISY UP…EMBRACING U-TURNS

🌹

"They got up and returned at once to Jerusalem." Lk.24:33

*H*ow many times have you been traveling down a highway and realized you needed to turn around? You see a break in the highway but you hesitate when you see a sign that says no u-turns. Perhaps you look to see if any police are around and then decide whether or not to give it a try. The only reason we make a u-turn is if we realize we are going in the wrong direction. No one wants to be off course. Our God doesn't play by the world's rules. Our God allows u-turns.

A few years ago I saw an incredible but true story aired on television one evening. It was a car accident involving some students from Taylor University in Indiana. A semi-truck lost control and hit their van. Five students were killed and one young woman was clinging to life. She was mistaken for Laura

Van Ryn. Her friend Whitney was assumed dead. The families were heart broken. The Van Ryn family stood at the bedside of their daughter praying for a miracle while the Cerak Family held a funeral for their daughter with 1400 people attending. It was five weeks later when the mistaken identities were discovered revealing that Whitney was alive and Laura was dead. Can you even begin to imagine the drastic u-turns each family had to make after this revelation? Hopes shattered and hopes restored. The precious gift of life and the absence of life. Imagine the Cerak family discovering that their daughter was not dead, but was alive. Imagine the Van Ryn family discovering that their daughter was not alive, but dead. It seems incomprehensible that anything like this could happen. But it did. What a journey!

Our story from scripture today is about another journey that takes a u-turn. The story is told in *Luke 24:13-35*. You might consider that this story isn't just about two disciples 2000 years ago, walking on the road to Emmaus. It's about you and me and the road we're walking on. It's about the direction we are taking. It's about our encounter with Jesus and the u-turns we take in our life. A u-turn can be a defining and transforming time in our life.

STARTING OUT

We see two disciples starting out on a journey on Resurrection Sunday. They are leaving Jerusalem, which to the Jews was a place of promise, purpose, and presence. They were on the way to Emmaus, which means "obscure" people despised. It was a seven mile trip which equaled two or three hours of walking. They were leaving Jerusalem because their hopes had been completely shattered. They had left everything to follow Jesus. They put their hopes in him as the one who would save Israel from the oppression of Roman rule. Instead, he

was scourged, crucified, died, and was buried. Even though there was rumor that the women found the tomb empty and angels said he has risen, they still left, without waiting to see what would happen. Isn't that like us too? We despair of life's circumstances from time to time and we lose heart when our expectations have not been met. We become disappointed, discouraged, and defeated. So what do we do? We leave and give up too soon. We walk away from God, from loved ones, and from our difficult circumstances.

ENCOUNTERING JESUS

The two disciples were walking and discussing the events of the last week in Jerusalem. They were struggling with doubt, confusion, and skepticism.

As they are walking a stranger joins them on the way, but by a supernatural act of God, they were restrained from recognizing him. Even so, they were too engrossed and preoccupied with their own sadness and dashed hopes. How many times do we also fail to recognize Jesus because we are too focused on our circumstances, trials, hurts, and pain. Even in their grief, Jesus sought them out. He knew their hearts, their disappointments, and wanted them to return to him. Jesus also seeks us out. He appears out of nowhere and shows us the way.

Jesus asked the disciples what they were discussing. They find it baffling that he doesn't know about the events of the past week. In our day, it would be a prime time news story splashed all over television, facebook, and twitter. The disciples tell him all about Jesus, their hopes and dreams, and the horrific events of the past week. It is at this time that Jesus calls them foolish and slow of heart. He says, "Did not Christ have to suffer these things and so enter into his glory?" *Luke 24:26.* Beginning with Moses and all the prophets he explained what was said in all the scriptures concerning himself. These disciples knew the word of God but didn't apply it to their own circumstances. We do that also. We know the Word of God but we forget to apply it to our particular trials and circumstances.

There was something about the interaction with this stranger that intrigued them. Their hearts were stirred and they were moved by the conversation. When he pretended to move on, they urged him to stay. It was in the breaking of bread that they finally recognized him. They said, "Were not our hearts burning within us while he talked with us on the road and opened the scriptures to us?" *Luke 24:32.* Jesus reveals himself to us in the same way. When we break bread together and when we open the Word, he speaks to us and helps us understand the mysteries of life. How long has it been since you've felt that stirring in your heart? He's with you at this very moment. You can ask him now and he will reveal himself to you.

MAKING A U-TURN

"They got up at once and returned to Jerusalem." Luke 24:33

Even though it was a late hour and probably dangerous, the two disciples didn't wait. They didn't procrastinate, doubt, or analyze the situation. They made a quick u-turn back to Jerusalem to tell the disciples. Although this was the same road it was a different road. A road once marked with defeat, despair, and hopelessness was now a road with hope restored, spirits lifted, and joy supreme.

If the road you're on is taking you in the wrong direction, you too can make a quick u-turn. If your hopes and dreams have been shattered and broken, you can make a u-turn. If you make that decision today, you will have a life-changing encounter with Jesus. Is that what you want? Just turn around—he's waiting for you. He'll walk with you and counsel and guide you as he did with the disciples on the way to Emmaus. This is a walk you can take today!

Daisy Up Exercises:

Get some newsprint or drawing paper. Draw a divided highway. Draw a stick figure of yourself walking down the road. Make some signs that might indicate you are walking the wrong way. What speaks of that in your life right now? Then draw yourself making a u-turn on the other road. Make some signs that show you are now going in the right direction.

Give a name to the destination on your first highway…then name the destination on your u-turn highway.

Find a few verses from scripture that will encourage you to keep going in the right direction. Write them out at the bottom of your picture.

Journal Prompt:

Finish this prompt. Write for 15 minutes without stopping. Let the story flow without trying to force it. Here's the prompt: He (she) suddenly made a u-turn...

Prayer:

Lord, I know that you direct my steps on the right path. I'm noticing some signs along my journey that are telling me to turn around, go a different way, try something new. I trust that your Word will be a light on my path guiding my steps. Help me to make u-turns in the areas of my life that are not pleasing to you. I want every step I take to bring me closer to you and to your purpose for my life. I ask this in Jesus name. Amen.

Quote:

"We are not human beings on a spiritual journey. We are spiritual beings on a human journey." Stephen Covey

AFTERWARD

*D*ear Readers, I want to say **KUDOS** to all of you for fin-
ishing this 30 day journey of Daisy Up. I hope that your
Daisy Up encounters with God were times of light, grace, peace
and insight. I pray that you know God's favor is established all
over you. He wants to:

- *Bless you*
- *Deliver you*
- *Comfort you*
- *Heal you*
- *Strengthen you*
- *Release you*
- *Embrace you*
- *Fill you with His Love, Mercy, and Compassion*

*This incredible journey has just begun. If you and I continue
to Daisy Up—beginning our day in God's Embrace, there's no*

limit to what He will do in us and through us. We will experience a deeper meaning and purpose for our life. I pray that God stirs your heart with a passionate love for Him. I pray that He gives you visions, dreams, and a future full of hope. Thank you for the honor of sharing these 30 precious days with you. But let's not stop here. Let's begin again tomorrow to Daisy Up in God's Embrace. Are you with me?

"Don't forget to pray today because God did not forget to wake you up this morning."
Oswald Chambers

CPSIA information can be obtained at www.ICGtesting.com
Printed in the USA
BVOW010331110113

310342BV00003B/10/P

9 781625 091215